"Emerson is not only one [...] coming scholars, but on[...] This fine little book is evid[...] [...] of that."

"Crisp, clear, and engaging, *Between the Cross and the Throne* briefly and competently examines the frequently misunderstood and often avoided book of Revelation. Readers will enjoy it and find themselves understanding much about Revelation's content, genres, imagery, narrative, theology, and message."

"Christians often avoid reading Revelation because it either scares or confuses them—or both. Fret no more! Matthew Emerson has written a fantastic commentary on the most fantastical book of the Bible, balancing scholarly study with on-the-ground Christian life. *Between the Cross and the Throne* is a helpful and hopeful primer on Revelation for the layperson, the student, the pastor, the professor, and everyone in between."

"Emerson has done an invaluable service to the church by providing a clear and concise summary of the main themes of Revelation. He employs sound principles of interpretation to guide the reader in properly understanding Revelation's message. But Emerson doesn't leave the reader in the text of the ancient world. He also includes thoughtful and pointed application of the text. This book is a great introduction to the book of Revelation."

BETWEEN THE CROSS AND THE THRONE

THE BOOK OF REVELATION

Other titles in
the Transformative Word series:

BETWEEN THE CROSS AND THE THRONE

THE BOOK OF REVELATION

TRANSFORMATIVE WORD

MATTHEW Y. EMERSON

Edited by Craig G. Bartholomew

LEXHAM PRESS

Between the Cross and the Throne: The Book of Revelation
Transformative Word

Copyright 2016 Matthew Y. Emerson

Lexham Press, 1313 Commercial St., Bellingham, WA 98225
LexhamPress.com

Print ISBN 9781577996583
Digital ISBN 9781577997139

Series Editor: Craig G. Bartholomew
Lexham Editorial Team: Lynnea Fraser, Elliot Ritzema, Abby Salinger
Cover Design: Jim LePage
Back Cover Design: Brittany Schrock
Typesetting: ProjectLuz.com

TABLE OF CONTENTS

INTRODUCTION

In most Christian circles, the book of Revelation is either wildly popular or completely avoided. Some churches turn to it for clues about the end times, attempting to correlate their newspaper headlines with certain passages of John's Apocalypse or Daniel's visions. On the other hand, many Christians respond to Revelation with sentiments that mirror Dorothy's in the *Wizard of Oz*: "Dragons, beasts, and harlots, oh my!" However, this book is neither a decoder ring for the end times nor an avoidable, weird addition tacked on to the biblical canon. Rather, it is a book that was *and is* vital for the Church; it assures us, even as we face tribulation, of the triune God's victorious reign and the imminence of Christ's return.

Overview

John, who Church tradition has identified with John the Elder and the apostle, wrote Revelation late in life while in exile on the island of Patmos. In this book, John recounts a vision he received from the risen Jesus. Throughout, he urges readers to hold fast to their confession that Jesus is Lord in spite of opposition from Rome and Caesar. Most, if not all, of the book uses figurative images and language. For instance, John often refers to churches as "lampstands," angels as "stars," and Satan as "the Dragon." John draws these images primarily from the Old Testament, especially from the book of Daniel. These word pictures allow us to visually and imaginatively understand the fundamental conflict of the world—the war between God and Satan.

PATMOS AND THE SEVEN CHURCHES

John's vision begins with the image of the exalted Christ, who stands gloriously victorious in the midst of his churches (Rev 1:9–20). Jesus, who has already conquered Satan through his death and resurrection, then exhorts each of the seven churches that comprise John's audience to stand firm against all opposition—both spiritual and physical (Rev 2 and 3). John is then taken up into God's throne room, where he sees the entire people of God and all of creation worshiping God (Rev 4). The people also acknowledge Jesus as the Lamb who was slain and the Lion of the tribe of

Judah, the one who is worthy to open the scroll of God's judgment because of his death and resurrection (Rev 5).

OUTLINE OF REVELATION

1. Introduction (Rev 1)

2. Letters to the Seven Churches (Rev 2–3)

3. Visions of the Throne Room (Rev 4–5)

4. The First Cycle of Judgment: The Seven Seals (Rev 6:1–8:5)

5. The Second Cycle of Judgment: The Seven Trumpets (Rev 8:6–11:19)

6. The War of the Dragon and the Lamb (Rev 12–14)

7. The Third Cycle of Judgment: The Seven Plagues and Seven Bowls (Rev 15–16)

8. A Tale of Two Women: The Harlot and the Bride (Rev 17:1–19:10)

9. Armageddon and the End of All Things (Rev. 19:11–20:15)

10. The Renewal of All Things in the New Creation Kingdom of the Lamb (Rev 21:1–22:5)

11. Conclusion: Persevere in the Faith Because Jesus Is Coming Soon (Rev 22:6–21)

The rest of the book follows three cycles of God's judgment on his enemies—(1) seven seals (Rev 6:1–8:5); (2) seven trumpets (Rev 8:6–11:19); and (3) seven plagues or bowls (Rev 15 and 16). Each of these cycles shows God's judgment on those who do not follow

Jesus as king, but each cycle also demonstrates God's faithfulness and mercy. God is faithful to his people, who are represented by the 144,000 (Rev 7) and the two witnesses (Rev 11:1-14), and he is also merciful to the nations, as his judgment is intended not only to show his wrath but also to call all to repentance.

Revelation also includes two extended images of the struggle between the Church and the followers of Satan; these wars are figuratively depicted as being between a woman and the Dragon's servants (Rev 12-14) and between the Harlot of Babylon and the Bride of Christ (Rev 17:1-19:10). The final section of the book includes the battle of Armageddon (Rev 19:11-21), a description of the millennium (Rev 20:1-6), the final judgment (Rev 20:7-15), and the new creation (Rev 21-22).

The Theological Center of Revelation

Christians in the first century faced a variety of challenges, including religious rejection by the Jews, culture clashes with Graeco-Roman social practices, and outright political opposition from Rome. The situation today is not much different for many Christians around the world, particularly with the threat of persecution in biblical locales like Turkey and Iraq.

Revelation depicts trials as being rooted in the work of Satan, who attempts to draw people away from Christ and toward destruction. John, who personally experienced persecution and the power of the emperor, writes to remind his readers that God, not Satan, is ultimately sovereign and victorious. They therefore should remain faithful to Yahweh even while the enemy assaults them from every side.

John's first-century audience might have wondered amid persecution and the devastation of the world how the claim that "Jesus is Lord" could be true. We might wonder a similar thing today. And although we are often tempted to react to hardship and suffering by questioning God's good providence, John insists that God reigns supreme even in the midst of all of sin's effects. The fundamental proof of this is found in the person of Jesus, who is both the source of John's vision and its central character and message.

Jesus Christ took sin, death, and the grave on himself, thus suffering with and for his people on the cross, but he also decisively defeated the enemy in his victorious resurrection. He is "the faithful witness, the firstborn of the dead, and the ruler of kings on earth," the one "who loves us and has freed us from our sins by his blood and made us a kingdom, priests to his God and Father," and the one who "is coming with the clouds ... who will be seen by all, even those who pierced him" (Rev 1:5–7). Jesus' death and resurrection make up the two-part work that demonstrates his empathetic suffering as well as his victory over all rulers, principalities, and powers.

It is because Jesus, the second person of the Trinity in flesh, has died and risen that we, as believers, can hope in the midst of suffering, knowing we have both a high priest who has suffered like us and a victorious king who will one day crush his enemies. The Lion of Judah, who is also the Lamb who was slain, shows the people of God that they can overcome the evil one because he has already overcome death, hell, and the grave. We can stand firm because he has already stood firm, and we can fight the Dragon's servants because

Christ has already bound their master.

Further, this same Jesus will return again, when he will utterly destroy the one he has already defeated, the Dragon, as well as all the Dragon's followers. Then he will wipe every tear from all of his people's eyes and renew all things. This is the theological center of Revelation—because Jesus has already won the war on our behalf, and because he is coming again, Christians can stand firm even in the midst of persecution and temptation.

> We can stand firm because he has already stood firm, and we can fight the Dragon's servants because Christ has already bound their master.

SUGGESTED READING

☐   Revelation 4–5

☐   Daniel 7 and 12

☐   Revelation 21:1–8

Reflection

Do you tend to embrace or avoid reading Revelation? What factors have led to shaping your attitude toward this book?

_____

_____

_____

How is Revelation applicable to the entire Church?

_____

_____

_____

REVELATION AS LITERATURE

Today, many Christians avoid John's vision of the end of all things, most likely because of his consistent use of unfamiliar imagery and figurative language. Most of us, especially modern Western Christians, are simply not familiar with this type of literature. Our unfamiliarity with the Old Testament—from which John draws most of his imagery—coupled with modernity's focus on the objective and scientific, makes it difficult to grasp what John is doing in Revelation. For instance, Revelation 8-9 and its description of mutant locusts is difficult for modern readers to understand; in many cases, readers either avoid it and the book altogether or they try to make it match with today's headlines—and in this case, with current military technology. Yet John explicitly uses distinct literary devices, a narrative, Old Testament allusions, and specific genres to help us grasp what he is doing in the book. Instead of being a book to avoid or a contemporary prediction chart, when we understand John's methods, Revelation can be seen for what it is—a testimony to the Triune God's work in Christ. Understanding how John uses each of the literary devices mentioned will allow us to further explore the theological message of individual passages and the entire book. In other words, we need to understand John's work as literature in order to understand it narratively and theologically.

Genre

To better interpret Revelation, let's first look at its genre—or genres, since John uses at least three different genres throughout the book. Revelation is a letter, a prophecy, and an apocalypse.[1] As we read and seek to understand Revelation, it helps to grasp the significance of these literary genres and the specific literary devices associated with each of them.

> **GENRE**
>
> The term "genre" refers to the category of literature in which a book can be placed. For instance, types of genres in Western literature include poetry, novels, epic, mystery, historical fiction, science fiction, comic book, and so on. As with Western literature, biblical literature can fall into a variety of genres. Identifying the genre or genres of a book can be helpful in determining what types of literary devices the author will use.

Letter

The book of Revelation is written as a letter to seven churches in Asia Minor (modern-day Turkey).[2] This letter-like quality can be seen primarily in the introductory material (Rev 1–3) and the conclusion (Rev 22:6–21). John exhorts his audience in the middle of the book (e.g., Rev 13:10) and ties Jesus' appeal to the seven churches to overcome (Rev 2–3) to specific events in the body of the book and to its conclusion in Revelation 21–22.

The details of the introduction and conclusion are particularly relevant for understanding the book's character as a letter.[3] John's opening address (Rev 1:1–8) and concluding plea (Rev 22:6–21) are both strikingly similar to the introductions and conclusions of other New Testament letters.

GREETINGS IN NEW TESTAMENT LETTERS AND REVELATION

Rev 1:4	"Grace to you and peace from him who is and who was and who is to come …"
Col 1:2	"Grace to you and peace from God our Father."
Rom 1:7; 1 Cor 1:3; 2 Cor 1:2; Gal 1:3; Eph 1:2; Phil 1:2; 2 Thess 1:2; Phlm 3	"Grace to you and peace from God our Father and the Lord Jesus Christ."
1 Thess 1:1	"Grace to you and peace."
Titus 1:4	"Grace and peace from God the Father and Christ Jesus our Savior."
1 Pet 1:2	"May grace and peace be multiplied to you."
2 Pet 1:2	"May grace and peace be multiplied to you in the knowledge of God and of Jesus our Lord."
Jude 1:2	"May mercy, peace, and love be multiplied to you."

Much like we see in Paul's letters, John's introductory material is expanded in the body of the book and repeated in the conclusion.[4] And like the General Letters that immediately precede Revelation in the New Testament, John continually emphasizes testing, perseverance, rejecting false teachers, and overcoming.[5]

What does this tell us about Revelation, and particularly about how to read it? First, it tells us that John had a particular audience in mind. Historically, the audience was made up of seven particular churches with specific theological and ethical situations that needed to be addressed. These churches were experiencing repeated persecution by a number of different groups. They were not only persecuted by the government, but by false teachers who constantly attempted to infiltrate their congregations. The Jews who had rejected Christ also rejected them. In addition, they were immersed in the Graeco-Roman culture, which exhibited different morals and encouraged alternate religious beliefs. Thus, the Christians from these seven churches were continually tempted by false teaching, pleasure seeking, and persecution to stray from Christ and his teaching. They were confronted with a choice between the power of God and the power of Satan, manifested in doctrinal, social, and political ways.[6] John had a specific message for this audience: Remain faithful to the Almighty Triune God until the end.

Second, because the number seven symbolizes universality in Revelation and other apocalyptic literature, it is highly likely that John also wrote his book with a more universal audience in mind. The fact that

John writes to seven churches is probably an indication that he intends Revelation to be an exhortation not only to these seven specific churches but to God's entire Church throughout space and time.[7] Certainly there are indications that John is speaking against Rome in his book, but this apocalyptic and prophetic letter is intended for all believers, whether they are citizens of the first-century Roman Empire, residents of 21st-century China, or anything in between.

Prophecy

Revelation also falls under the genre of prophecy, and John patterns his book after the ministry of the Old Testament prophets. For instance, his prophetic call in Revelation 1:10–19 (repeated in 10:1–11) resembles the prophetic calls of Ezekiel, Isaiah, and Daniel. Both of Revelation's visionary prophecies, as well as the oracular prophecies in the midst of those visions (e.g., Rev 7:14–17; 14:8–10), are patterned after Isaiah, Jeremiah, Ezekiel, and Zechariah.[8] John also connects his vision to the message of the Old Testament prophets through a literary device called "recapitulation": John seeks to summarize and consolidate the message of all the Old Testament prophets in his own book through the use of figurative images.[9]

This is important to note as we read Revelation because, although many readers think of the future when they hear the word "prophecy," John has a much more comprehensive scope in mind. The Old Testament prophets did not speak only of the future but of the past and the present as well. They were concerned not only to speak to Israel and the nations about what *will* happen but also about what God had *already done* for them, to them, and through them, and therefore how they should respond to him at that moment.

The prophets wanted Israel and the nations to understand all of time in relation to the rule of Yahweh, and this is no less true of John's prophecies in Revelation. John certainly speaks about what will happen in the future, especially in Revelation 20:7–22:5, but he also speaks about and provides the proper interpretation for what has happened in the past. The clearest example of this is found in Revelation 12:1–6, where John clearly uses figurative imagery to describe the birth and resurrection of Jesus Christ. But while there are references to both past and future in Revelation, like many of the Old Testament prophets, John is supremely concerned with speaking to his audience's present. For readers of Revelation, this is crucial. We need to read John's vision with an eye to the present of first-century Christians and to our own contemporary context. Any interpretation of the text that could be deemed irrelevant to or unable to be grasped by first-century readers is likely to be missing John's point.

Apocalypse

Finally, John's Apocalypse is just that—an apocalyptic book. This means at least three things.[10] First, apocalyptic literature is typically presented as a vision given to the author through angelic intermediaries. This does not mean we should doubt that John really had a vision given to him by God's messengers, but it does mean that John intentionally connects his book to the apocalyptic genre by using this and other common apocalyptic literary devices.

Second, apocalyptic books tend to make heavy use of figurative imagery. In Revelation, this includes abundant use of Old Testament images as well as a symbolic use of numbers.[11] As we read Revelation, then, we need to understand how John intends to convey theological truths using those symbolic images. For instance, the two witnesses in Revelation 11 symbolize the church and its martyr-testimony to the world about Jesus Christ.[12] Instead of seeking to discern two specific men who will stand outside the temple in Jerusalem in our future, it is more appropriate—given the apocalyptic genre of the book and John's repetitive use of imagery—to focus on the spiritual and theological significance of these images and the message they are intended to convey.

Third, apocalyptic books focus on the end of history. The question of Revelation is: "How will Yahweh deal finally and completely with sin, death, and Satan?" In other apocalyptic books, this is wrapped up in Yahweh's final judgment—a judgment that occurs with his return to Israel at the end of time. For John this is no less true, but the difference is that John sees Yahweh's return and eschatological—that is, end times—act of salvation in two stages: the first and second coming of Christ. The end of history begins with Jesus' life and work and ends with his bodily return. There is thus an already/not yet tension to this eschatological climax, and John is primarily concerned with how to live in between the times, between Satan's defeat in the death and resurrection of Christ and his final destruction at Jesus' return. While John certainly

REVELATION AS LITERATURE 15

speaks of what we often think of as "the end"—Jesus' return and final judgment (Rev 20:7–22:5)—he is predominantly concerned to urge his readers to live in this present, when Satan has fallen but has not yet been utterly destroyed (Rev 12:7–17).

These three genres—letter, prophecy, and apocalypse—give the reader clear indications of John's audience and purpose. While John is certainly writing a situational letter to a first-century audience and encouraging them to persevere as they face particular trials, his use of prophecy and apocalyptic imagery indicate that he intends his message to be read, believed, and followed by all Christians, then and now. For Christians in the first or twenty-first century, the application of Revelation is the same: Stand firm in the Lord Jesus Christ, come what may from God's enemies, because the Trinitarian God will make all things right when Christ returns.

> For Christians in the first century or twenty-first century, the application of Revelation is the same: Stand firm in the Lord Jesus Christ.

Literary Devices

Another tool in reading biblical literature is to identify the literary devices used by the author; these often closely relate to genre. In John's case, both the prophetic and apocalyptic genres support three important literary techniques that are vital to understanding Revelation.

Recapitulation

The prophetic genre provides John with a technique known as recapitulation. This literary device seeks to take earlier material, in this case from Old Testament books, and summarize and conflate them. The most prominent example of this is found in John's picture of the Harlot of Babylon (Rev 17–18). In John's description of her, he draws on the language and imagery used by various Old Testament prophets to describe Israel's many enemies—Tyre, Sidon, Babylon, and Egypt.[13] A similar situation occurs in the judgment cycles, when John draws mainly from the plagues of Egypt, but also from other instances of God's judgment in the Old Testament (e.g., the locust swarm in Joel 1:4).[14] John is attempting to describe events related to God, his people, and his enemies by conflating and summarizing the vast array of imagery found in Scripture. When reading Revelation, then, it is important not only to be familiar with Old Testament figurative imagery but also to realize that John is saying that the events depicted in his book are the consummation of all of that imagery—the final recapitulation to which they prophetically point.

Figurative Imagery

The apocalyptic genre provides the other two key literary devices employed by John: figurative imagery and symbolic numbers.[15] The latter is essentially a subset of the former, but will be discussed separately here. The clue to the entire book, the key at the top of Revelation's map, is recognizing that John uses pictures to describe reality throughout the book. In the center of the map key stands Revelation 1:20.

After describing Christ holding seven stars in the midst of seven lampstands, Jesus tells John, "As for the mystery of the seven stars that you saw in my right hand, and the seven golden lampstands, the seven stars are the angels of the seven churches, and the seven lampstands are the seven churches." John could not give us a clearer indication that his vision is a pictorial drama, and that to understand this visual story we must grasp his use of symbols. At the very least, here we are told that lampstands equal churches and stars equal angels.

Another key passage for understanding John's imagery is Revelation 12:1-6. Here John describes the story of a woman giving birth to a child and being pursued by a dragon. Revelation 12:4-5, and especially the reference to ruling "the nations with a rod of iron" (see also Psa 2:9), indicate that the child is the Messiah Jesus, which would identify the woman as Mary. But because this description of Mary is figurative—"a woman clothed with the sun, with the moon under her feet, and on her head a crown of twelve stars" (Rev 12:1)—we need to look closer at the imagery. We also see in this passage that Satan is described as a dragon who sweeps away stars, and again we need to remember John's use of imagery—such as the stars representing angels in Revelation 1:20—in seeking to understand this description.

As we read Revelation, then, it is crucial to understand the images as John uses them and not simply to assume that they are speaking only about modern-day events that have no relevance to John or his audience. For instance, instead of saying that the locust plague unleashed by the fifth trumpet in Revelation 9:7-11 refers to Apache helicopters, we ought to instead seek to discern the universal theological truth conveyed by this image that was still historically relevant to John's first-century readers.

Numbers

Alongside this figurative imagery, John also uses numbers symbolically.[16] This was a standard practice in apocalyptic works and was also used by the Old Testament prophets. The first place we see this numerical symbolism is where Jesus uses the number seven in his explanation of the stars and in the image of the lampstands (Rev 1:20). The Old Testament authors and other apocalyptic writers use the number seven to indicate universality. When Jesus speaks of seven churches, then he is speaking of not just seven individual churches but also the entire Church of God. Likewise, the seven particular congregations that

SIGNIFICANT NUMBERS IN REVELATION AND WHAT THEY SYMBOLIZE

Number	Represents
2	the number of witnesses in the Old Testament
3	the Trinity (or its opposition)
4	creation
6	man, and possibly imperfection
12	wholeness or completion, especially of the people of God

John writes to, and that Jesus sends messages to, are representative of the universal Church of God.

In sum, to interpret Revelation we need to engage it as John wrote it—figuratively and symbolically. Recognizing John's use of symbols and images does not negate the book's truthfulness—far from it. Instead, Revelation describes reality using word pictures, and so our job as readers is to reorient our imaginations—our beliefs about the world and its powers—through understanding and appropriating John's vision in our own day. When we are faced with the threat of martyrdom, the prospect of economic ruin, or even ridicule for our Christian faith from the larger culture, Revelation reminds us that, in spite of the uncomfortable or even dire nature of our present circumstances, the good and sovereign Trinitarian God is working all things together for good for those who love him.

Reflection

How does Revelation 1:20 and its explanation of the stars and lampstands help us understand the rest of the book?

_____

_____

_____

Revelation is a letter for a specific audience, one that is both historical and universal. How does this change the way you read and understand the book?

_____

_____

_____

THE DRAMA OF REDEMPTION

Narrative and Structure

Although Revelation is often identified by three genres, we could add a fourth: narrative. In Revelation, John tells a story—the story of Christ's victory over Satan, sin, and death in his first and second coming. The narrative style is most evident in Revelation 12–14. But John also appears to see his book as the completion of the entire biblical narrative, connecting Christ's work in his first and second coming with the story of creation and the fall (Gen 1–3).[1] In particular, John's vision of the new heavens and new earth in Revelation 21–22 is the consummation of Christ's work of redemption to restore and renew creation from the effects of the fall.[2]

In telling this drama of redemption—in which the Triune God rescues his people and his entire creation through the work of the incarnate Son—John uses a repetitive and interlocking structure.[3] After introducing the book in chapter 1, recounting Jesus' message to the churches in chapters 2–3, and describing the throne room of God in chapters 4–5, most of the book is taken up with the subsequent judgment cycles that occur because Jesus is found worthy to open the scroll in chapter 5. These cycles are repetitive, and so the events described in Revelation are not necessarily chronological; several times John tells the same story, ending at the same point, but using different imagery. The easiest way to see this repeating, interlocking structure is to examine the passages describing the last seal, trumpet, and bowl in each of the judgment cycles.

> **The Sixth Seal (Rev 6:12-17)** When he opened the sixth seal, I looked, and behold, there was a great earthquake, and the sun became black as sackcloth, the full moon became like blood, and the stars of the sky fell to the earth as the fig tree sheds its winter fruit when shaken by a gale. The sky vanished like a scroll that is being rolled up, and every mountain and island was removed from its place. Then the kings of the earth and the great ones and the generals and the rich and the powerful, and everyone, slave and free, hid themselves in the caves and among the rocks of the mountains, calling to the mountains and rocks, "Fall on us and hide us from the face of him who is seated on the throne, and from the wrath of the Lamb, for the great day of their wrath has come, and who can stand?"
>
> **The Seventh Seal (Rev 8:1-5)** When the Lamb opened the seventh seal, there was silence in heaven for about half an hour.

Then I saw the seven angels who stand before God, and seven trumpets were given to them. And another angel came and stood at the altar with a golden censer, and he was given much incense to offer with the prayers of all the saints on the golden altar before the throne, and the smoke of the incense, with the prayers of the saints, rose before God from the hand of the angel. Then the angel took the censer and filled it with fire from the altar and threw it on the earth, and there were peals of thunder, rumblings, flashes of lightning, and an earthquake.

The Seventh Trumpet (Rev 11:15–19) Then the seventh angel blew his trumpet, and there were loud voices in heaven, saying, "The kingdom of the world has become the kingdom of our Lord and of his Christ, and he shall reign forever and ever." And the twenty-four elders who sit on their thrones before God fell on their faces and worshiped God, saying,

"We give thanks to you, Lord God Almighty,
   who is and who was,
for you have taken your great power
   and begun to reign.
The nations raged,
   but your wrath came,
   and the time for the dead to be judged,
and for rewarding your servants, the prophets and saints,
   and those who fear your name,
   both small and great,

and for destroying the destroyers of the earth."

Then God's temple in heaven was opened, and the ark of his covenant was seen within his temple. There were flashes of lightning, rumblings, peals of thunder, an earthquake, and heavy hail.

The Seventh Bowl (Rev 16:17-21) The seventh angel poured out his bowl into the air, and a loud voice came out of the temple, from the throne, saying, "It is done!" And there were flashes of lightning, rumblings, peals of thunder, and a great earthquake such as there had never been since man was on the earth, so great was that earthquake. The great city was split into three parts, and the cities of the nations fell, and God remembered Babylon the great, to make her drain the cup of the wine of the fury of his wrath. And every island fled away, and no mountains were to be found. And great hailstones, about one hundred pounds each, fell from heaven on people; and they cursed God for the plague of the hail, because the plague was so severe.

There are at least two relevant connections between these judgments that help us to understand the structure of Revelation. First, each of these contains apocalyptic imagery that shows Yahweh's final end-times presence and judgment. This is especially evident in the language about hailstones, thunder, lightning, earthquakes, smoke, and fire. These images are indications of a theophany, or a "God appearing"—Yahweh has arrived.[4] In other words, these images are indications of Christ's second coming, or Yahweh's consummating presence on earth.

In addition, the sixth seal and seventh bowl are particularly instructive, as they both contain descriptions of islands and mountains fleeing from God's presence. This imagery speaks of the final, end-time judgment (i.e., the one found in Rev 20:7-15), or Yahweh's "holy war" against all those who rebel against him.[5] In each of these passages, as well as in the final judgment that begins in Revelation 20:11, we find creation fleeing from God. The silence in heaven that results from the opening of the seventh seal is also an indicator of final judgment. In the Old Testament Prophets, silence conveyed the sinful nations' inability to defend themselves before Yahweh's judgment, and so the silence of the entire world for a short period of time also points to judgment—and particularly that final, end-time judgment (see Psa 65:1-2; Zech 2:13).[6]

Second, and perhaps more important, each of these final judgments, in their respective cycle of seven, applies to the entire world rather than to just a portion. In the first five seal judgments, only a fourth of the earth is affected; in the first six trumpets, only a third; and in the first six bowls, only those with the mark of the beast experience the effects of God's poured-out wrath. However, with the sixth and seventh seal, the seventh trumpet, and the seventh bowl, the whole world experiences those judgments. In other words, the final judgment in each cycle appears to be just that—*final*. Therefore, the first thing we can say about Revelation's structure is that the three major cycles of judgment in the body of the book seem to actually be describing the same reality using different imagery. These cycles (seals, trumpets, bowls) are bookended by Christ's death and resurrection (Rev 5:5–6) and the final judgment at his second coming (Rev 20:7–15).

In the midst of these three cycles of judgment, there is another indication of structured repetition. Either just before or after the final judgment in each cycle, John gives a vision of Yahweh's faithfulness to his people. In Revelation 7:1–17, God's faithfulness is pictured using the language of 144,000 and "every tribe, tongue, and nation"; in Revelation 11:1–14 the imagery of the two witnesses is used; and in Revelation 14, right before the final cycle of plagues and bowls, John repeats the 144,000 imagery and also visualizes God's great harvest at the end of time.[7]

What we have so far, then, is an introduction in Revelation 1–3, a picture of God's sovereignty in Revelation 4–5, and then repeated cycles of judgment intertwined with pictures of God's faithfulness in Revelation 6–11 and 14–16. What about the remaining sections, Revelation 12–13 and 17–22? These are primarily narrative, and whereas the rest of the book is repetitive visions, these chapters tell a story that has a beginning, middle, and end. Chapters 12 and 13 begin with Jesus' birth and ascension, tell the story of the Church's tribulation at the hands of God's enemies, and culminate with chapter 14 and God's final judgment.[8] Chapters 17 and 18 tell the story of the Church's counterpart, the Harlot of Babylon. Whereas the Bride is faithful and pure, the Harlot is enslaved to the Beast, unclean, and politically and sexually manipulative. After reminding readers in Revelation 19:1–10 of

the character of the Bride—of whom they are a part—
and of her Bridegroom, Christ the conquering king
destroys the Harlot, Beast, and False Prophet in the remaining portion of chapter 19. Revelation 20:1-6 then
summarizes all of Revelation 12-13 and 17:1-19:10, and
the final victory and subsequent judgment of Christ
resumes in 20:7-15. With the world purged of both
sin's source, the Dragon, and its effects, Christ renews
all of creation and dwells with his people in the new
Jerusalem/temple/garden for eternity (Rev 21:1-22:5).

Thus this narrative tells the
story of God and his people
from Christ's first coming
to his second, again urging
the Church to remain faithful until the end. Both the
interlocking and repetitive
judgment cycles as well as

> John's purpose …
> is to urge us to
> continue to love the
> Lord, even unto death,
> because he reigns.

this more chronologically oriented narrative give the
same message to the whole people of God. John's purpose in repeating these judgment cycles and narratives is to urge us to continue to love the Lord, even
unto death, because he reigns.

The Time of Tribulation: The Last Days

As we've seen through studying Revelation's genre,
literary devices, and structure, Revelation is not just
about the very end of time, but speaks to the situation of God's people throughout history. John makes
this clear not only through literary devices, but also
through explicit statements and Old Testament allusions.[9] Beginning in chapter one, John shows that his
vision will include events that have happened in the

past, present, and future. Revelation 1:19 reads, "Write therefore the things that you have seen, those that are and those that are to take place after this." Notice the threefold division of time in this passage—past, present, and future. It is also clear from what John writes in the rest of the book that he has this threefold division in mind. Revelation 12:1–6 is again key, as the story that John records there, which is clearly a reference to Jesus' death and resurrection, is quite obviously in John's (and his readers') past. This is crucial for readers of Revelation to understand, because so often we focus on the book as primarily a code that only has relevance for the final years of world history. But Revelation 1:19 and 12:1–6, along with a number of other passages, don't support this type of reading.

Another indication that John wants to help readers understand the past and present as well as the future is his quotation of Daniel 2:28 in Revelation 1:1, 19, and 4:1.[10] In Daniel 2, the prophet is clearly looking forward to the coming of the Messiah in "the latter

Daniel 2:28	Revelation 1:1, 19; 4:1
There is a God in heaven who reveals mysteries, and he has made known to King Nebuchadnezzar **what will be in the latter days**.	The revelation of Jesus Christ, which God gave him to show to his servants the things that **must soon take place**. ... Write therefore the things that you have seen, those that are and those that **are to take place after this**. ... "Come up here, and I will show you what **must take place after this**."

days," and John uses the phrase "after this" as a paraphrase of Daniel's "the last days."

The context of Daniel 2, as well as the explanation of "the last days" in chapter 12, indicates this end-time period is inclusive of the entire period from Jesus' first coming to his return. This correlates with the way other Old Testament prophets use the phrase "the last days." Throughout the Hebrew Bible, from Moses to Malachi, that phrase is used to speak about what happens in Christ's first coming—namely the restoration of God's people, the defeat of God's enemies, and the work of the Suffering Servant. (The Suffering Servant is described in Isaiah [esp. chapters 41–55] as the Messianic Servant of Yahweh who saves Israel and the nations from their sins through his atoning death and resurrection.)

What is still missing is the final judgment, which Revelation does reveal in detail, but it is not until the very end of the book. As we read Revelation, then, our eyes, ears, and hearts should be attuned to how its message was relevant to its original audience in its immediate context as well as to how it has been relevant to the church throughout time and is still today. Because John wants to explain to the people of God how to live in the last days, which extend from Jesus' incarnation to his second coming—and therefore from John's past[11] and present and into his future—we can be assured of its continued relevance to the entire people of God.

Finally, one of the theological messages of Revelation—that God is sovereign over all of history, past, present, and future—is one more indication that it is concerned not only with the future but with the past and present as well. John uses the phrase "the One who was and is and is to come" (Rev 1:4b–5a, 8; 4:8) and its variations (Rev 11:17; 16:5), as well as "I am the Alpha and the Omega, the Beginning and the End" (Rev 1:8, 17; 21:6; 22:13) to show his readers the scope of God's rule. He rules not only over the future but also over the past and present.[12] The present rule of God is particularly important for John, as his primary purpose in writing the letter is to encourage his readers to remain faithful to God *in their present circumstances* until Christ returns. As the Church is persecuted, tempted to succumb to the pleasures that are available to them, and consistently confronted by false prophets, John reminds them that God is the Lord over all of history, and particularly their present context. In the midst of their tribulation, God still reigns and will reign until the end.[13] Whether we are experiencing persecution from the surrounding culture or government or whether we experience tragedy or hardship through disaster, disease, or economic depression, God is good and continues to reign.

SUGGESTED READING

- ☐ Revelation 6–11
- ☐ Revelation 15–16
- ☐ Daniel 2
- ☐ Daniel 12

Reflection

How does knowing God is sovereign, even in the midst of struggles, strengthen your faith in him?

_____

_____

_____

How does your knowledge of each of the genres of Revelation (letter, prophecy, apocalypse) affect how you approach the book? Can you name a modern example of how knowing a work's genre affects how that work (like a book, movie, or painting) is understood and interpreted?

_____

_____

_____

THE PORTRAIT
OF GOD AND
HIS PEOPLE

John's Picture of God in Christ

The dramatic story of Revelation includes three primary players: the Triune God, his people, and his enemies. By far the most important of these is the first,
and in particular it is the incarnate second person of
the Trinity—the Lord Jesus Christ—who functions
as the protagonist. At its heart, Revelation is a story,
and its main character is the crucified and risen Lord.
Jesus is the object of John's initial vision; he is the one
who moves the action forward through judgment and
salvation, and he consummates his work of redemption at the end of the book.

Noting Jesus' prominence in Revelation is not a
denial of the prominence of the Trinity; rather, the
Son's incarnation is the means by which the Triune
God accomplishes salvation. John emphasizes the uni-
fied operation of the three persons of God throughout Revelation, from the throne room scenes of both
Father and Son in Revelation 4 and 5, to the Son's

atoning work as validation for his ability to pour out both judgment and mercy in Revelation 6–11, to the Spirit's role in faithfully sealing and carrying believers through the tribulation in Revelation 12–14.

John's emphasis on the Triune God's activity for the Church conveys three fundamental truths about God. First, God is present with his people, the Church. We see this especially in Revelation 2 and 3, where Jesus sends his angel messengers to remind the Church of his presence through the Spirit and of their covenant responsibility to endure to the end. The Triune God in Revelation is also the ruling and reigning God, the one who sits on the throne in Revelation 4 and 5 and thus rules over all of history. He is the Lord over all creation, both in his care for it and use of it in judgment.[1] The third truth about God in Revelation is that he is God the Savior; he is the one who brings judgment and mercy to the nations, the one who brings down the great Dragon through the work of the Son and Spirit (Rev 12 and 20), and the one who will make all things new at Christ's return (Rev 21–22).

All of these actions are centered on the person and work of Jesus, and this is why John frequently focuses on Christ—beginning with his vision of the glorious Son of Man in chapter 1, which draws the readers' attention to Daniel 7 and Jesus' reference to himself as the Son of Man in the Gospels, and ending with his vision of Christ the King in the new heavens and new earth in Revelation 21 and 22. From start to finish, Revelation centers on the Alpha and the Omega, the author and perfecter of our faith (Heb 12:2).

This focus is seen especially in the coupling of two aspects of Jesus' identity: he is both Suffering Servant and Risen Lord. Jesus is portrayed as the Lamb who was slain (Rev 5:6). The crucified Lord is the one who is able to open the seals of the scroll of God's judgment (Rev 6), the one who overthrows Satan (Rev 12), and the one who consummates his work of new creation because he has already paid the price for it with his own blood (Rev 21:5–6). Jesus is also portrayed as the Lion of Judah and the Root of David (Rev 5:5). He is the ruling king who is able to open the scroll of judgment not only because he was slain but because he rose again, conquering death, hell, and the Dragon (Rev 12:1–13). Jesus is the Rider on the White Horse, the Savior of his Bride, who destroys all the enemies of God by casting them into the lake of fire (Rev 19:11–20:15). And he is the Alpha and Omega, the Beginning and the End, and the one who sits on the throne in the center of God's new city in his new creation, ruling over it forever (Rev 21:1–22:6).

These images of Christ, which visually articulate Jesus' death and resurrection, are intended to spur the Church to faith in their crucified and risen Lord, the King who has conquered death by swallowing it up in his own and who, raised by the Spirit, also raises us to new life in him. When facing the assault mounted by God's great enemy, God's people can stand firm because Christ has already done so on their behalf.[2] Whether we are facing temptation or trials or persecution, Jesus has already defeated sin, death, and Satan, and so by the Spirit we too can resist sin.

> When facing the assault mounted by God's great enemy, God's people can stand firm because Christ has already done so on their behalf.

We can have hope in the midst of trials, and stand firm in our faith in the face of persecution.

Images for God in Revelation

As noted in chapter 2, throughout Revelation John relies on figurative images to make his theological points. In his portrayal of God, we find both figurative imagery and theological language. One of the most important images for understanding John's vision of God comes in Revelation 4 and 5. John connects his vision of the throne room of God to his "last days" timeline through the phrase "what must take place after this" (Rev 4:1; compare 1:1, 19). In other words, this picture of God describes his rule and reign right now, in the time between Christ's first and second coming. John's vision is primarily focused on God's authority, and this is seen through his use of a number of Old Testament images. The most obvious of these is the centrality[3] of the throne on which God sits; this is an image that the Old Testament often uses to demonstrate the unparalleled and unshared authority of Yahweh.[4] John also describes Yahweh as appearing like "jasper and carnelian,"[5] which signifies God's unparalleled divine glory.

John uses three images to describe Yahweh's rule over his enemies, his people, and his creation.[6] John seemingly uses the imagery of a "sea of glass, like crystal" (Rev 4:6) to show that God is sovereign, even over those who oppose him. In the Old Testament, the sea represents chaos and evil (see Psa 74:12–17), and in the rest of Revelation, it is the place from which evil arises (Rev 13:1). In the new creation, the sea no longer exists (Rev 21:2). Therefore, the image of God sitting on or over the sea shows his authority over chaos and evil.

Similarly, John uses the image of the 24 elders sitting on 24 thrones in their white robes to depict Yahweh as the sovereign king of his people. With this image, John emphasizes God's sovereignty over his own people—the 24 elders, probably 12 representing Israel and 12 representing the Church. Likewise, the image of the four creatures around Yahweh's throne depicts him as Lord over all of creation; the creatures likely represent the fullness of creation (represented both by the number four, which is the number of creation,[7] and by the diversity of the creatures). Both creation and the people of God fall down before him, singing, "Worthy are you, our Lord and God, to receive glory and honor and power, for you created all things, and by your will they existed and were created" (Rev 4:11). John emphasizes God's dominion over every realm of creation, from the birds of the air and beasts of the field to his redeemed people and even to his enemies. John highlights Yahweh's rule over all things because John is exhorting the Church to remain faithful to the end, even in spite of persecution.

The Seven Spirits of God

However, when describing God, John is not generically monotheistic;[8] he is thoroughly Trinitarian. The Holy Spirit is spoken of a number of times as "the seven spirits." The first instance of this appears in Revelation 1:4-5,[9] where John greets the churches with grace from the Father ("him who was and is and is to come"), from the Spirit ("the seven spirits who are before his throne"), and from the Son ("and from Jesus

Christ the faithful witness"). Three other times in the book John also uses "seven spirits" to designate the Holy Spirit (Rev 3:1; 4:5, which also uses "seven torches of fire"; and 5:6, which also uses "seven horns and seven eyes"), since the number seven indicates universality and also, at times, perfection. At times, John also more directly references the Spirit (Rev 1:10; 2:11, 29; 3:13, 22; 14:13; 17:3; 21:10; possibly 19:10 and 22:6).

These descriptions of the Spirit indicate that he is the one who speaks to the churches (Rev 1:10; 2:11, 29; 3:13, 22; 14:13) and who gives the words of prophecy to John (Rev 19:10; 22:6). He is also the one who "carries" John into the different parts of his vision (Rev 17:3; 21:10). The references to seven, coupled with the imagery of fire and eyes, as well as the spatial references of "to and fro throughout the earth" (Rev 1:4–5; 3:1; 4:5; 5:6) suggest that it is particularly the Spirit through whom God's omniscience and omnipresence operate. This is not to say that the Father and Son are not also omniscient and omnipresent, but that it is primarily through the Spirit that God acts on these traits. In addition, the description of the Spirit as "before the throne" speaks to his participation in the Godhead, along with the Son "at the right hand" of the Father.

The Lamb and Lion

John also employs significant imagery that directly relates to the second person of the Trinity,[10] the incarnate Son. Through these images, we are reminded primarily of Christ's current victorious reign—beginning in Revelation 1 with John's vision of the Son of Man (Rev 1:9–20). John introduces Jesus immediately prior to this using a number of kingly terms (Rev 1:4–8), and then in his vision gives greater detail about this Jesus who "rules over the kings of the earth" (Rev 1:5). The vision is replete with Old Testament images that are reserved for Yahweh alone, and particularly the titles "Alpha and Omega" and "the first and the last" (Rev 1:17; 22:13). These are allusions to Isaiah 44:6 and 48:12, passages that speak of Yahweh as Creator—an act that is reserved for him and him alone.[11] Jesus' self-designation as the Creator is a claim to divinity. In addition, the pictures of fire, the sun, and whiteness all signify Yahweh's glory—a glory he does not share, but that Christ possesses. These images therefore further remind us of the Son's full divinity as the second person of the Trinity. Images of fire and the sun and a two-edged sword, along with Christ's placement in the midst of the seven lampstands and his grasp of the seven stars, point to Jesus' complete sovereignty over everything—from creation, to his people, to all nations, to the angelic beings.

Throughout Revelation, John continues to remind us of Christ's universal rule—from descriptions of Jesus in the letters to the seven churches (Rev 2–3), to Jesus' entrance as the Lion of Judah and Root of David in Revelation 5:5, to Christ's authority to open the seals of judgment and to command the angels to blow the trumpets and pour out the bowls and plagues. John also seems to be describing Jesus as a "mighty angel" in Revelation 10, where he is described as having full authority over creation ("he set his right foot on the sea, and his left foot on the land"; Rev 10:2), as able to sound the seven thunders (Rev 10:3), and as "wrapped in a cloud, with a rainbow over his head," and having a face like the sun and legs like pillars of fire (Rev 10:1). This language matches the description of Christ in Revelation 1:9–20 as well as in Revelation 5. The authority indicated by the rainbow (see Rev 4:3) and his stance over all of creation is coupled with his ability to speak judgment in the seven thunders. Once again, these images emphasize Jesus' authority.

Christ's eternal and comprehensive rule is also mentioned in Revelation 11:15; 12:5, 10–11; and 17:14. His authority culminates with his final judgment of the nations and the enemies of God, seen especially in Revelation 14:14–16; 19:11–21; and 20:7–15. Here Jesus is the one who harvests the earth, throwing the chaff of unbelieving nations into eternal fire. He is the conquering king who leads his people to victory against God's enemies, and he is the Judge of all the earth who puts a final end to Death, Hades, the False Prophet, the Beast, and the Dragon.

John's vision of Christ's rule is consummated in Revelation 21–22. Here we see Christ reigning eternally from his throne, along with the Father and the Spirit, over his enemies (Rev 21:8), his people (Rev 21:3–4), and over the renewed and restored creation (Rev 21:1, 9–22:5). While his rule has always been comprehensive, here we see it consummated, as sin, death, evil, Satan, and the enemies of God are completely destroyed and cast out of God's kingdom. Christ's reign is no longer invisible to the naked eye and seen only provisionally through his body, the Church. It is now seen by all flesh, and those who are redeemed through his death and resurrection reign with him in the new heavens and new earth for eternity.[12]

John's Picture of God's People

Closely related to Revelation's portrait of the Triune God, and particularly of Christ, is its portrait of God's people. Remember that John's primary goal is to encourage believers to stand fast in the midst of persecution and temptation. His portrait of God, who is the ruler of the entire universe even in the midst of tribulation, is intended to encourage perseverance among the people of God. In other words, because God is faithful to his Church in Christ, we can be confident and remain faithful even while facing intense suffering. Jesus' comments to the churches of Smyrna and Pergamum in Revelation 2:10, 13 and 14:12, and especially his call to endure, exemplify this purpose and John's message to God's people.

The refrain of Jesus in the letters to the seven churches, "To the one who conquers," also reminds the church that they are being called to persevere.[13] John's conclusion in Revelation 21–22 sees that those who conquer receive what they were promised in these first three chapters. As the letters to the seven churches—especially those to Sardis, Pergamum, and Thyatira—indicate, there are many churches on the brink of unfaithfulness. John urges them to persevere and not to fall away. Those who conquer, who remain faithful to the Triune God during the current tribulation, will dwell with God for eternity in the new heavens and new earth. John writes to remind the Church of this great truth.

With this purpose in mind, John's description of the Church can be summed up by Revelation 1:4b–5— "To him who loves us and has freed us from our sins by his blood and made us a kingdom, priests to his God and Father, to him be glory and dominion forever and ever. Amen." John says here that the Church is washed with the blood of Christ and reigns with him in his kingdom as his priests. These two images characterize much of how John describes the people of God in the rest of the book.

The Church is the redeemed people of God from all tribes, languages, and nations (Rev 7:9). The entire people of God is possibly indicated by the "twenty four elders" in Revelation 4:4; 11:16; and 19:4. This number is made up of two groups of twelve—one representing the tribes of Israel, and one representing the apostles. This is also exemplified in John's numbering of the "sealed from every tribe of the sons of Israel" at 144,000 (Rev 7:4, 9; 14:1). As with most of the language in Revelation, this number is figurative. By multiplying the two twelves together and then multiplying again by 1,000 (a number symbolizing innumerability), John may be indicating that the Church is true Israel—an Israel that is made up of all those who are united to Christ, both Jews and Gentiles.[14]

IMAGERY FOR THE CHURCH

John uses five main images to depict the Church as God's redeemed people:

(1) They are clothed in white robes.

(2) They drink from the water of life.

(3) They have been sealed with the name of God and have their names written in the book of life.

(4) They follow Jesus' commands.

(5) They are the bride of the Lamb.

The people of God are clothed with white robes, which, according to Revelation 7:13-17, means that they are the "ones coming out of the great tribulation," who have "washed their robes and made them white in the blood of the Lamb" (Rev 7:14). In other words, the white robes indicate that their wearers are believers in Christ, those who have repented of their sins, who have trusted Christ for forgiveness, and who have been made new by his Spirit (Rev 4:4; 6:11; 7:13-17; 19:8; 22:14).[15] The people of God are also the ones who have come to quench their thirst by drinking from the water of life, without payment (Rev 21:6; 22:17). John also refers to believers as those who have been sealed on their foreheads with the name of God (Rev 7:4; 9:4; 13:8; 14:1; 22:4) and who have had their names written in the book of life before the foundation of the world (Rev 13:8). Both of these images assure believers that their salvation, accomplished by Christ and applied by the Spirit, is secure because of God's great power. Believers are also those who follow the commands of Jesus, keeping themselves pure and blameless (Rev 14:4-5). This includes not only in their individual morality, but also their corporate holiness in the face of economic and political corruption (see the description of the Harlot in Rev 17-18).

Last, John refers to the Church as the Bride of the Lamb (Rev 19:6-10; 21:2, 9), which is partly intended to contrast her with the Harlot of Babylon in Revelation 17 and 18. John also combines this last image of the Bride with the new Jerusalem, the holy city coming down from heaven (Rev 21:2).[16] Although this might seem confusing, John regularly uses multiple images to describe the same reality. In this case, he uses both

Bride and new Jerusalem language to describe the Church, and in doing so is essentially saying that the people of God are made by God, purified by God, and blessed to spend eternity with God.

John also describes the Church in Revelation 4:5b-5 as reigning with Christ. As with the first description of the Church as redeemed, John uses a number of different images throughout the book to convey this point. He starts and ends the body of his vision by picturing 24 elders (representative of the whole people of God) with crowns on their heads and sitting on thrones (Rev 4:4; 20:4, 6). The thrones and crowns signify authority to judge under Christ. This is an authority that Christ has already given to his people by raising them up to the heavenly places, the place from which he rules, with him (Eph 1:20-21; 2:6). Of course, their rule is subjected under Christ's, as is indicated by the casting off of their own crowns (Rev 4:10) and the waving of palm branches (Rev 7:9). This recognition of Christ's ultimate authority, even as they are given authority under him, is also indicated by their worship of God in Christ (Rev 4:11; 5:8-14; 7:10-12; 11:16-18; 14:3; 15:3-4; 19:1-5). In each of these instances, believers worship, testifying to who God is and what he has done in Christ.

Testimony is not easy, though, and throughout Revelation testimony is seen primarily through the lens of martyrdom (Rev 6:9-11; 12:11, 17; 14:13; 17:6; 20:4). While the saints pray, symbolized by incense going up before God's throne (Rev 5:8; 8:3-4), this prayer is mingled with cries of "How long, O Lord?" (Rev 6:9-11). To serve God and not the idolatrous Dragon is to take up your cross and follow Christ, even to death.[17]

John uses two complementary images in the middle of the book to make this point. In Revelation 11, John describes the Church as two witnesses, also referred to as two olive trees and two lampstands. Even though the Dragon and the other enemies of God persecute the Church for a symbolic 42 months, the Church continues to testify to the Lord's work, even to the point of martyrdom. But God demonstrates his faithfulness by raising them from the dead after three and a half days—a reference to his faithfulness to Christ in raising him from the dead. The work of Christ is the demonstration of and grounds for God's faithfulness to those who are in Christ.[18] The second image John uses is that of the woman and her offspring fleeing into the wilderness. God nourishes the woman and her offspring there, protecting them from the Dragon, for 1,260 days—the same time period that the two witnesses stand in front of the temple.

Like John's call to holiness, his call to martyrdom continues to be a timely one. Today, brothers and sisters in Christ are still being killed for the sake of their Savior, and countless more are oppressed economically and politically because of their faith.

The goal of this testimony is to dwell with God for eternity (Rev 21:3–4, 22; 22:3–5, 14), sharing in Christ's reign as his vice-regents. We see this particularly in the phrase "those who conquered" (Rev 15:2; 21:7). For enduring believers, the promise is that we will share eternally in Christ's presence and rule, dwelling with the Triune God as his image bearers throughout all the earth. Our status as a kingdom of priests will be consummated at Christ's return. This should give believers hope in light of the trials and temptations we face, and especially in light of the intense persecution of Christians happening in many parts of the world.[19] As men and women face mockery, beatings, and death for testifying to the work of Christ, Revelation gives us hope that Yahweh will not let one of his sheep be snatched from his hand (John 10:29) and that he will execute perfect justice at Christ's return.

SUGGESTED READING

- ☐ Revelation 1:12–18
- ☐ Revelation 5:5–6
- ☐ Revelation 12:1–6
- ☐ Revelation 21:22–27

Reflection

What are some specific ways that the Church can remain holy in spite of the many sinful economic and political practices promoted by the current culture?

_____

_____

_____

How do Jesus' life, death, and resurrection give Christians confidence to remain faithful when facing trials, suffering, and persecution?

_____

_____

_____

THE PORTRAIT OF GOD'S ENEMIES

In contrast to God's faithfulness to his people and their steadfast faith in him, the enemies of God depicted in Revelation are unfaithful and deceitful. Revelation's description of God's enemies is one of complete contrast: God and his people are the opposite of the Dragon and his followers. We see this in what could be described as an "unholy Trinity" of the Dragon, the Beast, and the False Prophet. However, these three are not actually a Trinity; they are not one being in three persons. Rather, their unity in purpose—to make war on the people of God and to mock Yahweh—makes it appropriate for John to contrast their evil nature and destructive work with God's holiness and saving acts.

> God and his people are the opposite of the Dragon and his followers.

We also see God's followers contrasted with the Dragon's followers, recapitulated as the Harlot of Babylon. Therefore, the unholy Trinity is a deceptive mockery of the true and only Triune God, and the Harlot is a deceptive mockery of Christ's Bride.

46

By using this imagery, John is reshaping his readers' imaginations so that they will be able to remain faithful in the context of the Roman Empire.

The Unholy Trinity

The Dragon

John's first detailed depiction of the Dragon is in Revelation 12:3-4, 9. It is clear from this description and others elsewhere that the Dragon represents Satan, the prince of the power of the air (Eph 2:2), and the accuser and enemy of God. Here and in the rest of Scripture, Satan spearheads the world's rebellion against God, leading both the host of fallen angels and those human beings who reject God as their king. He is presented in Revelation as a mocker of God the Father, the first person of the Trinity. This is especially clear in John's description of the First Beast in Revelation 13:1-10, where the Dragon gives life and authority to the First Beast, the Dragon's image. This mocks the Father's granting of life and authority to the Son in his resurrection and ascension, as well as the Son's status as the image of the Father.

The Dragon's authority over the rebellious world is seen especially in his seven heads and ten horns. Revelation 17:7-14 explains this imagery: the seven heads represent seven hills and the ten horns represent ten kings. While these images probably allude to Rome,[1] they are also Old Testament images for earthly authority and the kingdoms of the nations (see Dan 7:4-8, 20, 24).[2] The specific numbers of seven and ten, or seventy if multiplied (a common practice when dealing with symbolic numbers), may be a reference to the "Table of [Seventy] Nations" in

Genesis 10.[3] The Dragon is thus portrayed as the ruler of the powers and principalities of the temporal and rebellious kingdoms of this world, in contrast to Yahweh and his comprehensive and eternal kingdom. Although the Dragon is thrown down by the death and resurrection of Jesus (Rev 12:1–12),[4] he still "makes war" on the followers of Jesus (Rev 12:13–17), primarily through deploying his Beast and False Prophet.

The Beast

The Beast rises from the bottomless pit (Rev 11:7), which is synonymous with the sea (Rev 13:1), and makes war on Christ's Church. He is a mockery of God the Son in three ways.[5] First, he is in the image of the Dragon. Like Satan, the Beast has seven heads and ten horns, and each head has a blasphemous name written on it (Rev 13:2). These blasphemous names are a counterfeit of Christ's forehead, which has the name of God written on it (Rev 19:12); the ten diadems, or crowns (Rev 13:2), are counterfeits of Christ's many diadems (Rev 19:12). Thus, while Christ is the image of God, the Beast is the image of the Dragon.

These pictures of the Beast's reign, namely his horns and diadems, emphasize the second contrast between the Beast and Christ: their rulership. While Christ rules over God's people, the Beast rules over God's enemies (Rev 13:4, 7–8). The fact that the Beast is made up of a number of different animal images mocks Christ's reign over creation. We see this in the counterfeit of the four living creatures surrounding the throne in Revelation 4 and 5 as well as in the parallel with the rebellious beasts in Daniel 7:2–7.[6] The beasts in Daniel, like the Beast in Revelation, rebel against Yahweh's rule and seek to both oppress God's people and deceive the nations. The Beast in Revelation is also given a throne and great authority by the Dragon (Rev 13:2), much like Christ is given his throne and authority from God the Father. In addition, the title given to the Beast in Revelation 17:11, "the one who was and is not," is a counterfeit of Christ, who is "the one who was and is and is to come."

Third, the Beast mocks the saving work of Christ. The Beast is healed from a mortal wound, counterfeiting the death and resurrection of Jesus (Rev 13:3). He is also the one from whom the Second Beast/False Prophet derives his authority; the Beast sends out the Second Beast/False Prophet with his authority. This is a mockery of Christ's authority to send the Spirit (Rev 13:12).

It's also important to note that the Beast's number is 666 (Rev 13:18). This number is significant because the number six is less than seven—the number symbolizing perfection or completeness.[7] The number six also represents man, since mankind was created on the sixth day of creation. The three sixes may be a reference to the unholy Trinity. In other words, 666 is a symbolic number, much like the other numbers of Revelation, and likely symbolizes, at least in part, the Beast's imperfection, his place in the "unholy Trinity," and his representation of and authority over sinful humanity.

The Second Beast/False Prophet

The third person of Revelation's unholy Trinity is the Second Beast (Rev 13:12), also referred to as the False Prophet (Rev 16:13; 19:19). As the Dragon mocks the

Father and the Beast mocks the Son, the False Prophet mocks the Holy Spirit and counterfeits his work. The False Prophet raises the Beast from his mortal wound by breathing life into it (Rev 13:15), mocking the Spirit's raising of Christ from the dead (Rom 8:11). The False Prophet also performs signs that resemble the works of the Spirit (Rev 13:13), and causes people to follow the Beast (Rev 13:14). And the False Prophet marks the enemies of God on the forehead with the number of the Beast (Rev 13:16–17), while the Spirit seals the followers of God with the name of God on their forehead (Rev 7:3; 14:1; see also Eph 1:13).[8]

PORTRAIT OF GOD'S ENEMIES

Holy Trinity	"Unholy Trinity"
God the Father	Dragon
the Son	Beast
Holy Spirit	Second Beast/False Prophet

The Harlot of Babylon

Just as the Dragon, Beast, and False Prophet mock the true Trinity, the Harlot of Babylon makes a mockery of the Bride of Christ. These two women of Revelation are polar opposites, reminiscent of Lady Folly and Lady Wisdom in Proverbs 1–9. The Harlot is the symbolic figure representing all those who follow the Dragon, and so the descriptions of unbelievers throughout the book can be combined with John's description of the Harlot in Revelation 17–18 to give us a holistic picture of human beings who rebel against God. To see how the people of God and the enemies of God are contrasted throughout Revelation, we can compare Babylon and the Bride, and unbelievers and believers more generally.

Babylon vs. the Bride

The clearest summary of Revelation's description of unbelievers comes in John's picture of the Harlot of Babylon in Revelation 17–18. The whole host of human beings who reject Christ as their king are symbolically represented as a harlot, a woman who prostitutes herself to the Beast. This brings to mind the many prophetic passages in the Old Testament that describe both Israel and the nations as prostituting themselves to false gods (e.g., the book of Hosea).[9] The harlot's name, Babylon, is intended to remind readers of one of Israel's greatest enemies in the Old Testament—the one that took Israel out of the promised land and into exile (e.g., Jer 27). But John's description also draws from Old Testament descriptions of Tyre, Sidon, and Egypt (e.g., Isa 23:1, 5; Ezek 29:9–21), among others. This means that the Harlot can be understood as a recapitulative image of all of Israel's enemies. She is symbolic of every person and every kingdom that has ever and will ever oppose the rule of Yahweh.[10]

Particularly instructive is a comparison of John's descriptions of the Harlot in Revelation 17:1–6 with his depictions of the Bride in Revelation 14:1–5 and Revelation 19:6–10.[11] These descriptions highlight a few key ways the Harlot and the Bride are polar opposites of one another.[12] First, the two women's clothing stands in stark contrast. While the Harlot wears a multicolored robe and much jewelry, the Bride is arrayed in simple, white linen. In many contemporary cultures the bride still wears white to symbolize her sexual purity, and this is the same meaning it carries in Revelation (see Rev 14:4).

The Harlot, on the other hand, is arrayed as a prostitute, and her behavior confirms her occupation. To break down the symbolism a bit, John is essentially contrasting the sexual morality of believers with the sexually immoral practices of unbelievers. Again, this outward manifestation of sexual sin points to the root of all sin, idolatry, as indicated by the Harlot's name and her connection with Old Testament imagery regarding idolatry and adultery. The second way the two women are described in opposite ways is through their relationship to the world's political and economic powers. The Harlot seduces and is seduced by kings and merchants (Rev 17:18; 18:3), and she thus represents the fact that the unbelieving world and those who inhabit it are full of economic and political corruption.[13] The red color of her clothing, along with the description of the cup she drinks, also indicates her persecution of the saints.[14] Red is associated elsewhere in Revelation with persecution of Christians (Rev 12:3; 17:3), and the imagery brings to mind blood as well as wrath (specifically via the cup imagery; e.g., Isa 51:17; Matt 26:39). Here economic and political corruption ultimately point to her persecution of Christians. Believers, on the other hand, testify to their citizenship in the kingdom of God by being oppressed and martyred by these same kings and merchants. The Harlot lays with them while the Bride lays down her life in opposition to them. Finally, the Harlot and Bride have much different relationships with their consorts. The Beast, upon which the Harlot rides (Rev 17:3; a symbol of her impure sexual union), eventually destroys his consort (Rev 17:16), while the Lamb has a pure, undefiled, and eternal marriage to his Bride (Rev 19:6-10).

The Followers of the Beast

Related to John's description of the Harlot in Revelation 17 and 18 is his picture of unbelievers throughout the book. This connection is made explicit in Revelation 17:15 (compare 18:3), where the waters upon which the Harlot sits are identified as the unbelieving nations. In the same way that the Harlot is the opposite of the Bride, so the nations who follow the Beast are opposites of the chosen believers who follow the Lamb. This contrast is seen in several ways throughout Revelation. First, contrasting language is used in the judgment narratives. Unbelievers being judged are described as sexually and ethically immoral (Rev 9:21; 18:3), doing what is unclean and false (Rev 21:7), idolatrous (Rev 9:20; 13:11-18), and unrepentant (Rev 16:9, 11). Their actions, which are especially highlighted by their sexual behavior, are indications of their idolatry and unrepentant stance toward Yahweh. John pictures this through his use of "seal" imagery. Unbelievers "do not have the seal of God on their foreheads" (Rev 9:4), and instead are marked on the forehead and right hand with the number of the Beast (Rev 13:16-18). Unlike the Church, they do not have their names written in the book of life (Rev 13:7-8).[15]

Under the authority of the Beast (Rev 13:7-8), and because they are deceived by the False Prophet (Rev 13:11-18), the unbelieving nations make war on the Church. John vividly pictures this in Revelation 11, where the nations "trample the holy city under their feet" (Rev 11:2). The unbelievers' actions are turned on their heads in Revelation 14, where instead of trampling God's people they are trampled in the winepress of the Lamb (Rev 14:20). This final judgment—along with the final battle between the Lamb and Gog and Magog (Ezek 38–39; see Zech 12–14; Zeph 3), who symbolically represent all the rebellious nations[16]—brings their warfare to an end. All unbelievers experience Christ's final judgment in the same way throughout the book, which we see especially in the final seals and trumpet and the seven bowls. Those who stand against Yahweh on earth not only experience physical harm but also are unable to stand in the presence of God's judgment (Rev 6:14–16). While the Church greets her Bridegroom at his second coming and dwells with him on the new creation for eternity (Rev 21:2–3), the followers of the Beast flee from his presence and are thrown into the lake of fire, where they experience for eternity the second death (Rev 21:8).

While these descriptions of God's enemies may seem either abstract or unrelated to the life of the believer, John makes his purpose clear in his letters to the seven churches. The warnings to the churches of Pergamum, Thyatira, and Sardis all contain language that mirrors the descriptions of the unholy Trinity and especially the Harlot. John warns Pergamum against false teaching and sexual immorality and reminds the Pergamum church of Christ's war against the enemies of Yahweh (Rev 2:14–16). The warning to the church at Thyatira is telling, since the description of Jezebel and the destruction that will come for those who follow her (Rev 2:20-23) sounds like the description of the Harlot and her followers (Rev 17). Finally, John's warning to the church at Sardis reminds readers of the contrast between believers, who have white garments, and unbelievers, who wear soiled garments.[17] In each of these contrasts, it is the Church who is pure and undefiled, while unbelievers are unrepentant, sexually immoral, and soiled by their sin. John warns these three churches in particular to flee from these practices and from the rebelliousness toward Yahweh that they signify. Destruction waits for those who do not turn from their idols and turn to the living God.

Again John's message is applicable for contemporary followers of Jesus. Today's Christians are bombarded with all the arrows the Enemy can fling, the same as those directed at believers in John's day. For example, sexual immorality is rampant in the West, promoted through pornography and perversion of God's design for marriage. It is to the point in some parts of Western culture that the Church has capitulated to the culture's ideas about sex and marriage, bowing to increasing peer and political pressure. But John calls Christians to stand firm against this tide of cultural compulsion, even if it means political fallout.

In other parts of the world, Satan's persecuting arrows are more prominent. Sometimes Satan uses local governments or cultures to cause economic hardships for Christians, and sometimes he uses political pressures, like laws against evangelism, to silence them. A current example is the economic struggle of many countries in the Global South, where low wages and harsh working conditions create oppression for those working in factories. These factories can also be means of temptation for other Christians, particularly business owners, who see profit and gain in oppressive economic practices. Still, John's call remains the same: The Church is to stand firm against these temptations. Destruction waits for those who remain coupled with their human-made gods.

John's Critique of Rome

For his original readers, John's depictions of the Unholy Trinity and the Harlot would call to mind specific elements of their life in the Roman Empire. John makes at least three implicit references to Rome in his book. The first two refer to the Roman Empire in general, and the third appears to refer to Emperor Nero in particular.

With respect to the empire as a whole, John's picture of the Harlot is especially telling. First, John's description of the economic corruption that occurs because of the world's relationship with the Harlot parallels some of Rome's economic practices. For instance, the list of cargoes sold by the Harlot in Revelation 18:12–13 would probably be seen by Revelation's original audience as "a feature of the newly conspicuous wealth and extravagance of the rich families of Rome in the period of the early empire."[18] John is thus critiquing one of the significant sources of power in the Roman Empire—the wealthy—by identifying their traded goods with the cargo of the Harlot.

A second and even more explicit reference to Rome comes in Revelation 17:9, where John says that the Harlot sits on seven mountains or hills. According to Richard Bauckham, "That Rome was built on seven hills was extremely well-known. By referring to its seven hills John was not concealing Babylon's identity but making it obvious."[19] For first-century readers of Revelation, John's message is clear: Making your bed with the Harlot means making your bed with the Roman political and economic machine.

John also appears to refer to Rome's Emperor Nero. In 13:14, the fact that the Beast has a mortal head wound and yet lives may reflect a myth about Nero that was popular in John's day.[20] Nero committed suicide with a sword in AD 68, after which there arose the legend of Nero's return, and this may be John's cultural reference in Revelation 13:14.[21] What John is doing, then, is using figurative imagery to critique the current political and economic situation while also universalizing his critique so that it will be relevant to all believers.[22]

In today's climate, John's critique of the Harlot hits home when we think of the many economic and political practices carried out both at home and abroad and their harmful and many times oppressive consequences. One thinks, for instance, of the relatively recent Jim Crow laws imposing segregation in the southern United States. In that case, many churches were complicit in this spiritual and physical abuse of fellow human beings and, in many instances, fellow Christians. Churches should avoid at all costs this kind of dalliance with the Enemy, lest they lose their lampstand and ride the Beast instead.

SUGGESTED READING

- ☐ Revelation 13
- ☐ Revelation 17

Reflection

How does understanding the unholy Trinity's mockery of the one, true God help us discern how Satan and his followers work in the world?

_____

_____

_____

How can today's believers heed John's warnings to Pergamum, Thyatira, and Sardis to flee from practices that resemble those of the Harlot of Babylon?

_____

_____

_____

THE WAR OF
THE LAMB

Time, Times, and Half a Time

Throughout Revelation we see again and again contrasts between the people of God and those who rebel against him. The root of this contrast is the conflict between God and Satan, a conflict that began with the Accuser's rebellion and subsequent temptation of Adam and Eve (Gen 3).[1] The war between the Lamb and the Dragon is the story of Scripture, and John seeks to summarize, symbolize, and demonstrate the culmination of that narrative in his book. The narrative of Scripture is summarized and completed by the narrative of Revelation.

Particularly, the story of Revelation is the story of the New Testament. Although Revelation draws on Old Testament themes and events, the book's time frame is especially structured around the events of Jesus' first and second coming. These two advents serve as bookends for what happens in Revelation, with the cross and empty tomb standing on one side and Christ's return in glory standing on the other. John uses a number of different symbolic numbers for this time period, including 42 months, 1,260 days, and "time, times, and half a time." Each of these speaks to the same period of time, and each is drawn from the book of Daniel. It is fairly easy to see how 42 months is related to 1,260 days, since they are different terms of measurement for the same value (42 [months] x 30 [days] = 1,260; so 42 months = 1,260 days). Thus in Revelation 11:2–3 John speaks alternatively of the enemies of God trampling the city for 42 months and the two witnesses proclaiming Christ for 1,260 days. These are the same time period.

This makes it easier to see the relationship between Revelation 11 and 12, since the woman, representing Israel, Mary,[2] and the Church all at once, is nourished in the wilderness for 1,260 days (Rev 12:6). In other words, the two witnesses stand in front of the temple for the same amount of time that the woman is nourished in the wilderness. This brings us to the third phrase John uses to describe the woman's time in the wilderness: "time, times, and half a time" (Rev 12:14). Here John equates 1,260 days with "time, times, and half a time."[3]

What, then, is the significance of these time periods? First, according to G. K. Beale, "The number 'forty-two months' is not literal but figurative for the eschatological period of tribulation repeatedly prophesied by Daniel (7:25; 9:27; 12:7, 11–12)."[4] In other words, 42 months and its variations in Revelation (three and a half years, 1,260 days) are references to the time of tribulation experienced by God's people in the last days.

The phrase "time, times, and half a time" also comes from Daniel 12:7. In this passage, Daniel asks the angel how long it will be until the end of all things, and the angel replies, "time, times, and half a time." Daniel 12:1-4 indicates that this measurement includes everything from the time of trouble until the final judgment. If we note from Mark 13 that the "time of trouble" (Dan 12:1) begins with Jesus' Passion,[5] then Daniel, and subsequently John, is using this phrase to describe the time between Christ's first and second coming—the church age. The War of the Lamb occurs in the time of the Church, who is his Bride, and lasts until his second coming and final judgment of his enemies.

The Dragon's Destructive Dominion

The sides of this war are clear-cut: There are those who follow the Lamb and those who do not. There is no middle ground, no Swiss neutrality. Those who oppose the Lamb are followers of the Dragon, who exercises his evil dominion over this world. In doing so, he "makes war" on the followers of God, primarily in three ways. First, he attacks the Church by tempting them with pleasure. The Harlot of Babylon provides the clearest example of this tactic, as her clothing and sexual immorality are means by which people are seduced.[6] Second, the False Prophet seeks to deceive through false prophecy. He uses both false signs and false teaching to mislead the world's population (Rev 13:13-14).[7] Third, the Dragon sics his Beast on the Lamb's Bride, attacking her through persecution.[8] Throughout Revelation, we see believers being killed by the followers of the Beast, and most notable are the stories of the witness and the woman in Revelation 11–13 (e.g., Rev. 11:7-8; 12:17; 13:7-8).

The Blood of the Lamb and the Seed of Woman

Throughout Revelation, God is active, particularly through his judgments in the seals, trumpets, and bowls, as well as in the final judgment. But just because he judges sinners doesn't mean he is simply an unloving bundle of fury. The destruction that John describes is actually intended by God not only to punish sin but also to call sinners to repentance. The conversion of the nations is Yahweh's goal.[9] While in Revelation 9:20-21 and 16:9, 11 the nations are unrepentant in the face of Yahweh's wrath, they are repentant in 11:13, and God even calls them to repentance in 14:6-13 and 18:4. Thus we should not conclude that God is pouring out wrath with reckless abandon, but that even in the midst of his righteous wrath toward sinners he is still seeking to convert them by warning them of their imminent destruction. Further, these judgments relate to the Exodus plagues and the new exodus themes throughout Scripture, suggesting that they are intended, like the exodus, to bring God's people out of slavery and into his kingdom.[10] Although plagues such as the turning of water into blood and swarms of locusts aren't pretty pictures, they are always accompanied by God's redemption of his people in the Old Testament (e.g., Exodus, Joel). Thus, while those who are unrepentant are judged, those who do repent are rescued.[11]

God's people are also active: through their willingness to be martyrs, Yahweh also conquers his enemies. The proclamation of the gospel and the conversion of the nations is his goal, both in the judgment of the nations and the martyrdom of his people.[12]

The Lamb's Judgment

The ultimate sign of God's activity is found in Christ, whose death and resurrection provide the foundation for God's righteous judgment toward the unrepentant, as well as the victory of his Church over the forces of darkness through their own martyrdom. We first see this in Revelation 5:6–10, where it is the Lamb who was slain who is able to open the scroll. Because the seals of the scroll, and thus the scroll itself, contain judgment, John is saying that Jesus is worthy to judge the nations because he has died on the cross. His victory over death gives him the right to judge those who follow the way that leads to death. John identifies explicitly his death and resurrection as the means by which Satan is thrown down (Rev 12:5–12), and it is through his death and resurrection that he gives life to and reigns with his saints for 1,000 years (Rev 20:4–6). Therefore, Jesus' death is the basis for his rule in Revelation.

The resurrection is also the key to the Lamb's reign in Revelation. Not only has Jesus taken death on himself, but he also has conquered it through the Spirit raising him from the dead. He is "the first-born from the dead, and the ruler of the kings of the earth" (Rev 1:5), "the living one" who has died and now lives forevermore. Because of his resurrection, he now holds the keys to Death and Hades (Rev 1:18). His authority over God's enemies, namely the Dragon, death, the grave, and the unbelieving nations, rests on his resurrection.[13]

The Testimony of the Church

We see Jesus ruling the nations with a rod of iron (Rev 1:5; 12:5) primarily through the judgments unleashed in the seven seals, trumpets, and bowls, and ultimately in the final judgment (Rev 14:14–20; 19:11–21; 20:7–15). He employs his angels (e.g., Rev 9:1–11) to pour out his wrath toward unrepentant sinners. But he also conquers through his Church, and this victory is won through martyrdom. Repeatedly we see believers being killed for their witness to Christ, but just as often we see them characterized as conquerors because of their faith in the face of death. In his seven letters, John urges the churches to conquer and to overcome (Rev 2:7, 11, 17, 26; 3:5, 12, 21). We quickly find out—through the vision of the Lamb in Revelation 5:5—that to conquer means to die in witness to Yahweh and in opposition to his enemies. This is clarified in Revelation 12:11, where it describes the Church as having "conquered [the Beast] by the blood of the Lamb and by the word of their testimony, for they loved not their lives even unto death."[14] Revelation 15:2 and 6:9 also speak of those who have conquered the Beast and his followers through their testimony.

The most detailed picture of the Church's witness to the supremacy of Yahweh through their martyrdom comes in Revelation 11, where the two witnesses, who symbolize the people of God, are killed for their faith. While God's enemies gloat for three and a half days (paralleling Jesus' three days in the tomb), the Spirit raises the witnesses to new life and thus demonstrates their victory over the Beast through their testimony. This is why Tertullian, a church father, could call the blood of Christian martyrs "seed."[15]

It is through believers being willing to be killed for their faith that God demonstrates his faithfulness to them and his power to save.

The End of the Age

At the end of history Christ will return in victorious battle, casting his enemies outside the new Jerusalem and into the lake of fire. The three judgment cycles (seals, trumpets, bowls) all end with this final judgment, described in detail in Revelation 14:14–20 and 20:7–15. Revelation includes two parts to Jesus' return.

First, the armies of the Dragon assemble at Armageddon immediately prior to the final judgment of the seventh bowl (Rev 16:16). This is fleshed out in Revelation 19:11–21, where John portrays the great and final battle of Armageddon, which occurs immediately prior to the final judgment of Revelation 20:7–15.[16] While the conflict in Revelation is one in which the enemies of God seem to conquer God's saints (Rev 11:7), in the end it is Christ's followers who are victorious through their testimony. Their victory is assured and consummated by the crucified and risen one, the Lamb who was slain, who now at the end of history returns as the conquering Lion of Judah. John's portrait of Jesus in Revelation 19:11–16 is striking. Here Jesus is revealed to the whole earth in all his glory, and for those who do not follow him it is a terrible sight. The descriptions John gives are taken from the Old Testament, although John also draws from New Testament language as well.[17] The sum of it is that Jesus is the righteous reigning king who triumphs finally and completely over all of God's enemies. He exercises his reign with a rod of iron against all who oppose him, striking them down with a sword coming from his mouth (see Rev 1:16; 2:16) and treading them in the winepress of his wrath. This latter image was foreshadowed in Revelation 14:14–20, where John speaks of the final harvest of believers and unbelievers in judgment terms, with unbelievers being trodden in the winepress and their blood rising to enormous heights.

Jesus and his followers here face all of the enemies of God, with the name Armageddon indicating symbolically the universal scope of the opposition.[18] We also see the Beast and the False Prophet destroyed, along with the kings of the earth who sat on the Harlot in Revelation 17. These images indicate again the totality of the destruction that is happening. While strict chronology is not John's goal, it appears from chapter 19 that the Harlot—representing unbelievers—is destroyed (Rev 19:1–2), and her destruction is immediately followed or perhaps is paralleled by the destruction of the rest of God's enemies (Rev 19:19–21). The only remaining enemy of Christ is the Dragon,

ARMAGEDDON

The origin of the name "Armageddon" is disputed, but it perhaps is a combination of "Har" (Hebrew for "mountain") and Megiddo, a place where Israel experienced opposition from a variety of enemies (see Judg 5:19; 2 Kgs 23:29; 2 Chr 35:20–22). Mountains are a common figurative image for kingdoms, and so this name perhaps figuratively represents all the kingdoms of the world who oppose the kingdom of God.[19]

and he is thrown into the lake of fire immediately prior to the final judgment (Rev 20:10).

The final judgment is the final act of warfare by Jesus, and it includes the resurrection of the dead, believing and unbelieving, and their eternal fate. Christ's basis for judgment is the book of life, and the whiteness of his throne indicates the truthfulness and justice of his decrees (Rev 20:11-12). For unbelievers, they along with Death and Hades are cast into the lake of fire (Rev 20:14). John refers to this as the second death, a direct contrast with the second resurrection of believers hinted at in 20:6.

After Christ's victory over all those who oppose Yahweh, restoration occurs and remains for eternity.[20] A new heaven comes down to a new earth, and on this new earth Yahweh dwells with his people (Rev 20:1-3). There is only peace, or shalom, here (Rev 20:3), because God in Christ has removed sin, its source, and all its effects from the world. The goal of creation—to dwell with God for eternity—is realized, and Christ reigns over and with his people forever (Rev 20:5-7). This new creation is not a second creation *ex nihilo*, but the culmination of the biblical storyline. What was lost in Genesis 1-2 through the fall in Genesis 3 has been redeemed, restored, and reconstituted through Christ's victory in Revelation 19-20 and his act of restoration in Revelation 21:1-2. Christ's payment for sin on the cross and victory over death in his resurrection result in the consummation

> After Christ's victory over all those who oppose Yahweh, restoration occurs and remains for eternity.

of the restoration of creation, with those who repent and believe in him dwelling eternally with God on the new earth as the new temple.[21] This is the eternal peace that comes after Christ is victorious over the powers of darkness. There is no more darkness, but only the light of the glory of God who dwells with his people (Rev 21:22-27).

SUGGESTED READING

☐   Revelation 12:7 –17
☐   Revelation 14:14–20
☐   Revelation 19:11–21
☐   Revelation 21:1–8

Reflection

Why is martyrdom considered a way to conquer in Revelation? What does this tell us about how God wants us to interact with those who are hostile to Christianity?

_____

_____

Why does John give such vivid and graphic descriptions of Jesus' victory over his enemies? How does he want us to respond to these pictures of Christ's rule?

_____

_____

_____

7

READING
REVELATION TODAY

Because we sometimes view Revelation like a fantasy
novel or an unbreakable Bible code, it can be challeng-
ing to see how it applies to us today. When most believers do search for relevance in this last book of the
Bible, it is often through trying to make their newspa-
pers match what they believe to be prophecies about
the very end of history. Going against this tendency
is the fact that John wrote Revelation for a specific
audience with a specific purpose, and we must understand this purpose if we want to understand what
Revelation has to say to our own context. Starting in
the first century and continuing throughout church
history, Revelation has always been immediately relevant to God's people in their present context without
recourse to a "prophecy watch" mentality.

John's use of universal language and figurative symbols indicate that his message is for the whole church
throughout space and time. Especially important here
is the use of the number seven in the beginning of the
book; because seven is a number signifying completeness or perfection, the seven churches symbolize the
universal church. While John certainly critiques his

own culture, he also intends for the book to exhort the entire people of God until Christ returns.

Antithesis

How, then, can we read Revelation today? One re-source for understanding Revelation's relevance comes from the concept of antithesis, made prom-inent by the Dutch theologian Abraham Kuyper. Revelation presents two options: serve God or the Dragon. In faith, sex, politics, or economics, there is no neutrality. A person can operate in these areas, which Kuyper called spheres, either faithfully or un-faithfully. The line down the middle, what splits faith-ful and unfaithful action, is called the antithesis.

When we think, then, about business or health care, we need to ask whether our thoughts and ac-tions in that sphere reflect a testimony to the Lamb or a capitulation to the domination of the Dragon and a partnership with the Harlot. Are we acting and think-ing in ways that testify to the freedom of the gospel of Jesus Christ and his lordship over all creation, or are we operating in ways that further the oppression and immorality fueled by Satan and his followers? For John, this meant critiquing Rome, giver of the good gift of *pax Romana*. For William Wilberforce and Frederick Douglass, it meant calling for an end to the abominable practice of chattel slavery in the midst of America's infancy and Britain's waning yet still power-ful empire. For Dietrich Bonhoeffer and other German Christians, it meant standing against Hitler's Nazi re-gime through the Barmen Declaration.[1] For contem-porary Christians, it may mean any number of things, such as working to end the oppression of women around the world who experience rape, violence, and neglect.[2] While we should not try to bind Christian consciences about specific political stances, we must remember that the call of Christ to take up our cross and die is not just a spiritual, otherworldly call but one that asks us to stand against the oppression and debauchery pervasive in our world today. Revelation also reminds us that oppression and debauchery are not only acts by individual people but often embedded in the structures of society. Standing against them many times means standing against popular culture and the current political powers.

FAITH IN ACTION

Voice of the Martyrs—an organization that tracks Christian persecution worldwide—shows through their prayer calendar and other resources that Christians around the globe are persecuted for their faith in Christ, not only through the threat of death but through economic and legal sanctions as well. Yet Christians are not willing to bend under the oppression of the local political, economic, and military powers. This is an example of what it might mean today to live on the faithful side of the antithesis.[3]

Elsewhere in the world faithfulness to the Lamb may not seem quite so dramatic, but it is firmly embedded in the drama of Revelation's story. Even when Christians simply have honest business practices or participate in social justice, if they are doing it out of faithfulness to Christ and for God's glory, they are acting on the right side of the antithesis. Thus to think about how Revelation is relevant today is to think about how we can glorify God and serve the church in every facet of our lives. Revelation is a wonderfully relevant book because it clarifies for us what the stakes are. Either be faithful to Christ or follow the Dragon to your own destruction. That is the choice every person has to make in Revelation, and it is the choice all of us have to make today.

Liturgy and Formation

One way we learn to make choices between the kingdom of God and the kingdom of this world is through the formation of our habits and desires. As James K. A. Smith has pointed out, what we love is shaped not only by what we learn with our minds but what we repeatedly do with our bodies.[4] The world has its own cultural liturgies,[5] whether it is indoctrinating Western culture into consumerism through the mall's blast of images and options[6] or implicitly pushing the pleasures of technology through caressing a screen repeatedly.[7] This is of course not to say that technology and shopping and the like are inherently evil, but that our practices regarding those resources and habits can shape us in alternate directions—either toward Christ or away from him. In the United States, children say the pledge of allegiance every day at the beginning of school, fans sing the national anthem at the beginning of every sporting event, and the country celebrates its independence every year with a national holiday. Westerners' annual, monthly, weekly, and daily calendars are filled with repetitive, and thus formative, habits and practices, and these shape their loves, desires, and dreams. What we do shapes who we are and what we want. The world has its own agenda in forming people, and it also has the practices to accomplish that purpose.

The church, therefore, must be intentional in providing alternative means of forming and shaping its people. Instead of shaping people to love idols, the church must shape people to love Christ. In doing so, God's people are also in a place to shape the world through living out their faith publicly and in all spheres of life. This means that local churches need to think deeply about

> Instead of shaping people to love idols, the church must shape people to love Christ.

their worship practices. Is their order of worship consistent? Does it promote love for Christ and his people, along with a willingness to testify to the Lord unto death? Does it combat the individualism, materialism, consumerism, and rampant sacred/secular dualism of today's world? While we do not want to usurp the role of the Spirit in convicting hearts and minds or add legalistic, extrabiblical requirements concerning worship services, local churches and their leadership should ask questions about their congregational worship, preaching, discipleship, and other ministries like, "Does the way we practice this mimic the wider culture, or is patterned after biblical practices? Are we promoting celebrity and consumerism in our music and teaching style, or are we pointing people to Christ?"

Revelation hints at this liturgical life of the church through implicitly mentioning a few of the early church's worship practices. John's vision begins on the Lord's Day and climaxes with the Lord's Supper

(Rev 19:1–10).[8] In the opening vision of God and Christ on the throne (Rev 4 – 5), there are hints of the procession, baptism, the Lord's Supper, preaching, prayers, and songs of praise.[9] These and other liturgical elements throughout the book indicate that John not only figuratively and theologically shows the choice believers have to make between following the Lamb or the Dragon, but that he also demonstrates the antithesis liturgically.

For believers today, this means our worship practices need to form and shape our minds and bodies to react faithfully to Christ when faced with persecution, pleasure, and false prophecy. One vitally important practice in the life of the church in this regard is the Lord's Supper. As the body of Christ remembers Jesus' Passion, we not only memorialize his victory for us but also proclaim it until he returns (1 Cor 11:26). The Supper reminds us of our past and looks to our future—when the Bride will dine with the Lamb (Rev 19:1–10), and both memory and hope give us power to live in the present. Because Christ has already defeated our enemy on the cross and in his resurrection, and because we know he will return in glory and victory, we can resist temptation and stand firm against persecution in the present.

Baptism likewise reminds us that our identity is not rooted in the kingdom of this world, but in Christ; our identity is grounded in his death, resurrection, and gift of the Spirit. As he died for our sins and rose to give us new life, so now we die to sin and rise to new life by his life-giving Spirit (Rom 6:1–4). Sin, death, and Satan have no power over us because we are citizens of Christ's kingdom, not the world's kingdom.

The preaching of the Word likewise is used by the Spirit to exhort and enable believers to live as God's image bearers, convicting them of sin and encouraging them toward faithfulness. Word and sacrament are both vital in the liturgical formation of Christians, shaping them to glorify God in Christ and reject the attacks and seductions of Satan and his followers. Other practices of the church—like prayer and the recitation of creeds or confessions—also shape and form believers to live faithfully in the midst of the attacks of the Accuser. As churches read Revelation, they ought then to consider how their worship practices will motivate and empower their members to live on the right side of the antithesis that cuts through every area of life.

> Sin, death, and Satan have no power over us because we are citizens of Christ's kingdom, not the world's kingdom.

SUGGESTED READING

- ☐ Ephesians 2:1–10
- ☐ 1 Peter 2:9–11
- ☐ Colossians 3:1–13

Reflection

Which church practices promote allegiance to Christ instead of to the Beast? Which church practices might promote consumerism instead of martyrdom?

_____

_____

_____

What are areas in your own life where you can think about being on the right side of the antithesis? Are there ways of thought, patterns of speech, or habits and actions you need to change in order to be a faithful follower of Christ in that area?

_____

_____

_____

8

CONCLUSION

Revelation is an exciting book, with its images of many-headed Dragons and Beasts, angels blasting judgment trumpets, and Christ returning in glory as the conquering king. Sometimes, though, these figurative images cause today's believers to shy away from John's Apocalypse because such images are simply unfamiliar to our modern imaginations. Throughout this study one goal has been to make Revelation more accessible by revealing what John wants to convey with his host of literary devices. When we recognize that his descriptions are symbolic (Rev 1:20), it is much easier to understand his message.

That message is simple: *remain faithful to God* in Christ by the power of his Holy Spirit *until he returns* in glorious victory over all his enemies. *Remain faithful until God returns.* John shows us that there are two and only two sides in the cosmic war that has been raging since Genesis 3: the side of Yahweh and the side of Satan. The question for readers of Revelation then is this: On which side will you stand? Revelation presented its earliest readers with this question in relation to the Roman Empire. Would first-century believers resist even unto death the seduction and oppression of the political and economic machine in Rome, or would they capitulate to it? The question remains the same for all believers throughout history. There is an antithesis running down the middle of every area of life, seen most clearly in political and economic structures. On one side stands faithfulness to Yahweh, and on the other stands following Satan. As Christians, this stark contrast must govern our decision-making, our thoughts, and our practices in every area of life.

Will we remain faithful as believers and as the corporate body of Christ, or will we fall prey to Satan's strategies of pleasure, persecution, and false prophecy? The local church must be on the forefront of this battle for every Christian's faithfulness, starting with worship practices. Does the local church, through the right preaching of the Word and the right administration of the sacraments, shape believers' loves and desires so that they resist the siren song of the world's pleasures? Does it form believers' loves and desires so that they are willing to be put to death for the sake of Christ and his gospel? These are the kinds of questions we need to ask ourselves as we read Revelation. There is a war going on, and John makes it clear that we need to be on the right side in our thoughts, in our speech, and in our actions.

> There is a war going on, and John makes it clear that we need to be on the right side in our thoughts, in our speech, and in our actions.

Of course, John does not leave us with a "pull ourselves up by our bootstraps" mentality. It is because

Christ has already been faithful, has already defeated the Dragon and his servants, has already conquered death and the grave, that we can stand faithfully with him and for him. Because he has raised us from the dead by his Spirit, and because his Spirit continually empowers us to faithfulness, we can be faithful to him. Perseverance in the faith is as much a gift of the Father through the Son and by the Spirit as our initial faith in Christ is. May God our Father grant us faithfulness to him in the midst of all of life's trials through the death and resurrection of his Son and by the power of his Holy Spirit. Amen.

NOTES

Chapter 2: Revelation as Literature

1. For a brief discussion of each of these three genres and how they are used throughout Revelation, see Richard Bauckham, *The Theology of the Book of Revelation* (New Testament Theology; James D. G. Dunn, ed.; Cambridge: Cambridge University Press, 1993), 1–17.

2. See Leon Morris, *Revelation* (TNTC; Grand Rapids: Eerdmans, 1987), 46.

3. Much of the following is abbreviated from Matthew Y. Emerson, *Christ and the New Creation: A Canonical Approach to the Theology of the New Testament* (Eugene, OR: Wipf & Stock, 2013), 143–47.

4. See G. K. Beale, *John's Use of the Old Testament in the Book of Revelation*, 300. Beale notes, for example, the parallels between the exhortation to the church at Thyatira to flee from Jezebel (Rev 3:18–29) and John's description of the harlot of Babylon in Revelation 18. Ibid., 311–16.

5. See Emerson, *Christ and the New Creation*, 145–47, for a more detailed explanation of the textual links between Revelation and these letters.

6. Emerson, *Christ and the New Creation*, xii–xiii; G. K. Beale, *The Book of Revelation* (NIGTC; Grand Rapids: Eerdmans, 1999), 171–72; Craig R. Koester, *Revelation and the End of All Things* (Grand Rapids: Eerdmans, 2001), 30–31.

7. The number seven is used by John to indicate universality. See "Literary Devices" for a discussion of John's use of numbers as figurative imagery. For the discussion of how seven churches indicate a universal audience, see Richard Bauckham, *The Climax of Prophecy: Studies on the Book of Revelation* (London: T&T Clark, 1993), 30.

8. Jan Fekkes, *Isaiah and Prophetic Traditions in the Book of Rev-*

elation: Visionary Antecedents and their Development (JSNTSup 93; ed., Stanley Porter; Sheffield: Sheffield Academic Press, 1994), 101–02.

9. Bauckham, *The Theology of the Book of Revelation*, 4–5; Beale, *John's Use of the Old Testament in Revelation*, 100, 109–10.

10. For a more detailed discussion on the apocalyptic genre, see David E. Aune, *Apocalypticism, Prophecy, and Magic in Early Christianity* (Grand Rapids: Baker Academic, 2006), 39–65; and Bauckham, *The Climax of Prophecy*, 38–91.

11. For more on how John uses these devices, see the "Literary Devices" section.

12. See Beale, *The Book of Revelation*, 556–620.

13. Bauckham, *The Theology of the Book of Revelation*, 20–21.

14. Bauckham, *The Climax of Prophecy*, 204–207.

15. For a more detailed discussion on each of these, see Baukham, *The Climax of Prophecy*, 30–38; Bauckham, *The Theology of the Book of Revelation*, 17–22; Beale, *The Book of Revelation*, 50–69.

16. Bauckham, *The Climax of Prophecy*, 29–37.

Chapter 3: The Drama of Redemption

1. Matthew Y. Emerson, *Christ and the New Creation: A Canonical Approach to the Theology of the New Testament* (Eugene, OR: Wipf & Stock, 2013), 151–60.

2. William Dumbrell, *The End of the Beginning: Revelation 21–22 and the Old Testament* (Eugene, OR: Wipf & Stock, 2001).

3. Craig Koester, *Revelation and the End of All Things* (Grand Rapids: Eerdmans, 2001).

4. Richard Bauckham, *The Theology of the Book of Revelation* (New Testament Theology; James D. G. Dunn, ed.; Cambridge: Cambridge University Press, 1993), 41–42.

5. G. K. Beale, *The Book of Revelation* (NIGTC; Grand Rapids: Eerdmans, 1999), 397–402.

6. Beale, *The Book of Revelation*, 451.

7. Notice once again how the seals and bowls mirror each other; islands and mountains flee at the final judgment(s), and

God's faithfulness is pictured using the number 144,000.

8. Note that chapter 14 serves as a bridge between Revelation 12–13 and 15–16, connecting God's faithfulness back to the narrative of the woman and the dragon and forward to the third judgment cycle.

9. For a detailed discussion of John's use of the Old Testament, see Beale, *The Theology of the Book of Revelation*, 76–99.

10. For more on how John uses Dan 2:28, see G. K. Beale, *John's Use of the Old Testament in Revelation* (Sheffield: Sheffield Academic, 1998), 165–91.

11. It might seem strange to talk of Revelation as referring to the past, but this is exactly what John does in a few places, particularly Revelation 12:1–5. Here John refers figuratively to Jesus' incarnation, death, and resurrection, all of which are in John's (and therefore the reader's) past.

12. See Bauckham, *The Theology of the Book of Revelation*, 23–30. Bauckham also points out that these phrases, and particularly "I am the Alpha and the Omega," help to provide structure for the book since they occur in the prologue, at the beginning of the vision, at the end of the vision, and at the conclusion. Ibid., 57–58.

13. Koester, *Revelation and the End of All Things*, 57.

Chapter 4: The Portrait of God and His People

1. Richard Bauckham, *The Theology of the Book of Revelation* (New Testament Theology; James D. G. Dunn, ed.; Cambridge: Cambridge University Press, 1993), 47–53.

2. Bauckham, *The Theology of the Book of Revelation*, 58.

3. Notice that in Rev 4:4 the throne is literally in the center of a circle. John uses geometric imagery as well as figurative imagery to communicate the centrality of Yahweh's throne.

4. For more on Yahweh not sharing his throne with anyone else, and thus for how it communicates his unparalleled authority, see Richard Bauckham, *Jesus and the God of Israel: God Crucified and Other Studies on the New Testament's Christology of Divine Identity* (Grand Rapids: Eerdmans, 2008), 152–81.

5. Jasper and carnelian are precious stones with reddish hues,

similar to rubies.

6. For more on these images, including the interpretations of them espoused here, and their Old Testament background, see G. K. Beale, *The Book of Revelation* (NIGTC; Grand Rapids: Eerdmans, 1999), 320–31.

7. As also used in the four corners of the earth and the four winds (Rev 7:1; 20:8). See Beale, *The Book of Revelation*, 322.

8. Monotheism refers to the belief that there is only one god. By "generally monotheistic" I mean that John does not just believe in the idea of only one god; instead, he believes in one particular God, the one God who exists in three persons, the Trinity, Yahweh.

9. On the Holy Spirit in Revelation, see Richard Bauckham, *The Climax of Prophecy: Studies in the Book of Revelation* (London: T&T Clark, 1993), 150–73.

10. David Aune demonstrates that the titles for Jesus in Revelation (e.g., "the Alpha and the Omega," "the first and the last") are intended to show his equality in essence, power, and authority with the Father. See his *Apocalypticism, Prophecy, and Magic in Early Christianity* (Grand Rapids: Baker Academic, 2006), 263–70.

11. See Bauckham, *The Theology of the Book of Revelation*, 54–56.

12. On Jesus in Revelation, including a more detailed explanation of the preceding paragraphs, see Bauckham, *The Theology of the Book of Revelation*, 54–65.

13. Craig Koester, *Revelation and the End of All Things* (Grand Rapids: Eerdmans, 2001), 54–57.

14. On the 144,000, see Bauckham, *The Climax of Prophecy*, 215–23. Bauckham suggests that the number not only represents the entire people of God but that, because of the use of tribes and numbers, it appears to echo Old Testament censuses. Those censuses were intended primarily for military purposes, and so John may be describing not only God's faithfulness in this passage but also his people's status as his army, fighting the Dragon through martyrdom.

15. Beale, *The Book of Revelation*, 934–44.

16. Bauckham, *The Theology of the Book of Revelation*, 127.

17. Bauckham, *The Theology of the Book of Revelation*, 90–94.

18. David L. Barr, "The Apocalypse as a Symbolic Transformation of the World: A Literary Analysis," *Int* 38 (1984): 39.

19. See Asia Bibi's story at http://www.aleteia.org/en/world/article/asia-bibis-final-plea-to-avoid-the-gallows-5901162817519616

Chapter 5: The Portrait of God's Enemies

1. For example, Rome was famously situated on seven hills. See Richard Bauckham, *The Climax of Prophecy: Studies on the Book of Revelation* (London: T&T Clark, 1993), 395.

2. G. K. Beale, *The Book of Revelation* (NICGT; Grand Rapids: Eerdmans, 1999), 878.

3. Bauckham, *The Climax of Prophecy*, 327.

4. Bauckham, *The Climax of Prophecy*, 186.

5. Bauckham, *The Climax of Prophecy,* 397.

6. Bauckham, *The Climax of Prophecy*, 193.

7. Bauckham, *The Theology of the Book of Revelation*, 16.

8. Bauckham, *The Theology of the Book of Revelation*, 114–15. Bauckham also notes the contrast between the False Prophet and the two witnesses of Revelation 11. Beale, *The Book of Revelation*, 707–11 suggests that the description of the Second Beast/False Prophet evokes the idea of apostasy and false teachers within the covenant community and not just someone on the outside.

9. For the Old Testament background on "Harlot," see Beale, *The Book of Revelation*, 884–85.

10. Craig Koester, *Revelation and the End of All Things* (Grand Rapids: Eerdmans, 2001), 156–57.

11. Even though Rev 14:1–5 does not specifically refer to the people of God, the 144,000, as the Bride, the parallels between the passages indicate that they are talking about the same group of people. Parallels include the voice like the roar of many waters and the sound of thunder and their clean linen garments. We could also add Rev 7, among other passages, to

this list of descriptions of the Bride.

12. Beale, *The Book of Revelation*, 855.

13. Beale, *The Book of Revelation*, 847–53.

14. Beale, *The Book of Revelation*, 854–55, 860.

15. Beale, *The Book of Revelation*, 715–18.

16. Beale, *The Book of Revelation*, 1022–24.

17. See Koester's discussion of these three letters in *Revelation and the End of All Things*, 61–65.

18. Richard Bauckham, *The Climax of Prophecy: Studies on the Book of Revelation* (London: T&T Clark, 1993), 352.

19. Bauckham, *The Climax of Prophecy*, 395.

20. Bauckham, *The Climax of Prophecy*, 407–31.

21. There is a second possible reference to Nero as well. Some interpreters have argued that the number of the Beast, 666 (Rev 13:18), may be a reference to Nero's name. For a discussion of this interpretation, see Bauckham, *The Climax of Prophecy*, 385–407.

22. Richard Bauckham, *The Theology of the Book of Revelation*, (New Testament Theology; James D. G. Dunn, ed.; Cambridge: Cambridge University Press, 1993), 35–39.

Chapter 6: The War of the Lamb

1. While the serpent is not explicitly identified with Satan in Gen 3, this interpretation has a long tradition in biblical and extrabiblical literature, including Rev 12:9. See also *2 Enoch* 31:3–6; *Apocalypse of Abraham* 23; *Apocalypse of Moses* 15–21; Wisdom of Solomon 2:23–24.

2. Wilfrid Harrington, *Revelation* (SP 16; Collegeville: The Liturgical Press, 1993), 29. See also William C. Weinrich, ed., *Revelation* (ACCS, NT 12; ed., Thomas Oden; Downers Grove: InterVarsity Press, 2005), 170–84.

3. For more on Revelation 12 and the time period it encompasses, see Matthew Y. Emerson, *Christ and the New Creation: A Canonical Approach to the Theology of the New Testament* (Eugene, OR: Wipf & Stock, 2013), 151–58.

4. G. K. Beale, *The Book of Revelation* (NICGT; Grand Rapids:

Eerdmans, 1999), 565.

5. For the relationship between Jesus' Passion and the "last days," see Peter Bolt, *The Cross From a Distance: Atonement in Mark's Gospel* (NSBT; Downers Grove: InterVarsity, 2004), 85–115. For the broader framework of how Jesus' life, death, resurrection, ascension, and gift of the Spirit at Pentecost inaugurate the Old Testament's expected "last days," see G. K. Beale, *A New Testament Biblical Theology: The Unfolding of the Old Testament in the New* (Grand Rapids: Baker Academic, 2011), 129–86.

6. Beale, *The Book of Revelation*, 854–56.

7. Beale, *The Book of Revelation*, 708–11.

8. Beale, *The Book of Revelation*, 680.

9. "The conversion of the nations" is Bauckham's phrase. See the chapter by the same name in Richard Bauckham, *The Climax of Prophecy: Studies on the Book of Revelation* (London: T&T Clark, 1993), 238–337.

10. Within Revelation the church is pictured as participating in a new exodus, particularly in Rev 12:13–17. See Beale, *The Book of Revelation*, 668–81.

11. Craig Koester, *Revelation and the End of All Things* (Grand Rapids: Eerdmans, 2001), 97–98, 102–103, 108–13, 137–41.

12. Koester, *Revelation and the End of all Things*, 108–11.

13. Richard Bauckham, *The Theology of the Book of Revelation* (New Testament Theology; James D. G. Dunn, ed.; Cambridge: Cambridge University Press, 1993), 56.

14. Bauckham, *The Theology of the Book of Revelation*, 88–94.

15. "We multiply whenever we are mown down by you; the blood of Christians is seed," Tertullian, *Apology*, trans. T. R. Glover and G. H. Rendall (Cambridge, MA: Harvard University Press, 1931), 50.12.

16. The issue of the timing of the millennium in Rev 20:1–6 will not be explored here. For an introduction to each of the major views, see Craig A. Blaising, Kenneth L. Gentry, and Robert B. Strimple, *Three Views on the Millennium and Beyond* (ed., Darrell Bock; Grand Rapids: Zondervan, 1999).

17. For a detailed explanation of these verses, and especially

the Old Testament background to which John alludes, see Beale, *The Book of Revelation*, 949–71.

18. Marko Jauhiainen, "The OT Background to *Armageddon* (Rev 16:16) Revisited," *NovT* XLVII, 4 (2005): 381–93.

19. See Juahiainen, "The OT Background to *Armageddon*," and Beale, *The Book of Revelation*, 840.

20. David Aune, *Apocalypticism, Prophecy, and Magic in Early Christianity* (Grand Rapids: Baker Academic, 2006), 275–79.

21. See G. K. Beale, *The Temple and the Church's Mission: A Biblical Theology of the Dwelling Place of God* (NSBT; Downers Grove: IVP Academic, 2004).

Chapter 7: Reading Revelation Today

1. Bonhoeffer also was involved in an assassination plot against Hitler. I do not include it here because Christians differ on the warrant for violence in political action.

2. Nicholas D. Kristof and Sheryl WuDunn, *Half the Sky: Turning Oppression into Opportunity for Women Worldwide* (New York: Vintage, 2009).

3. For an introduction to the types of events described in this paragraph, as well as to ways we can pray for and assist our brothers and sisters around the globe, see The Voice of the Martyrs website: www.persecution.com.

4. James K. A. Smith, *Desiring the Kingdom: Worship, Worldview, and Cultural Formation* (Cultural Liturgies 1; Grand Rapids: Baker Academic, 2009) and *Imagining the Kingdom: How Worship Works* (Cultural Liturgies 2; Grand Rapids: Baker Academic, 2013).

5. By "liturgy" I simply mean repeated and formative practices. While this term may be more familiar to some Christians, all churches have some practices that they repeat at each corporate gathering. We may call it "the order of worship," or not refer to it at all, but nevertheless every church repeats certain practices and concepts during their worship service each week.

6. Smith, *Desiring the Kingdom*, 19–27.

7. Smith, *Imagining the Kingdom*, 142–50.

8. For the idea that Revelation is broadly liturgical, see, e.g., G. K. Beale, *A New Testament Biblical Theology: The Unfolding of the Old Testament in the New* (Grand Rapids: Baker Academic, 2011), 797 n. 52; and G. B. Caird, *New Testament Theology* (Oxford: Oxford University Press, 1994), 184. Indeed, for Caird, "The Revelation of John begins on the Lord's Day and ends in Eucharist." Ibid.

9. Allen Cabaniss, "A Note on the Liturgy of the Apocalypse," *Int* 7.1 (1953): 78–86; and Jack Kilcrease, "Creation's Praise: A Short Liturgical Reading of Genesis 1–2 and the book of Revelation," *Pro Ecclesia* 21.3 (2012): 314–25.